V&R unipress

ZEITGESCHICHTE

Ehrenpräsidentin:
em. Univ.-Prof. Dr. Erika Weinzierl († 2014)

Herausgeber:
Univ.-Prof. DDr. Oliver Rathkolb

Redaktion:
em. Univ.-Prof. Dr. Rudolf Ardelt (Linz), ao. Univ.-Prof.[in] Mag.[a] Dr.[in] Ingrid Bauer (Salzburg/Wien), SSc Mag.[a] Dr.[in] Ingrid Böhler (Innsbruck), Dr.[in] Lucile Dreidemy (Wien), Dr.[in] Linda Erker (Wien), Prof. Dr. Michael Gehler (Hildesheim), ao. Univ.-Prof. i. R. Dr. Robert Hoffmann (Salzburg), ao. Univ.-Prof. Dr. Michael John / Koordination (Linz), Assoz. Prof.[in] Dr.[in] Birgit Kirchmayr (Linz), Dr. Oliver Kühschelm (Wien), Univ.-Prof. Dr. Ernst Langthaler (Linz), Dr.[in] Ina Markova (Wien), Univ.-Prof. Mag. Dr. Wolfgang Mueller (Wien), Univ.-Prof. Dr. Bertrand Perz (Wien), Univ.-Prof. Dr. Dieter Pohl (Klagenfurt), Univ.-Prof.[in] Dr.[in] Margit Reiter (Salzburg), Dr.[in] Lisa Rettl (Wien), Univ.-Prof. Mag. Dr. Dirk Rupnow (Innsbruck), Mag.[a] Adina Seeger (Wien), Ass.-Prof. Mag. Dr. Valentin Sima (Klagenfurt), Prof.[in] Dr.[in] Sybille Steinbacher (Frankfurt am Main), Dr. Christian H. Stifter / Rezensionsteil (Wien), Priv.-Doz.[in] Mag.[a] Dr.[in] Heidemarie Uhl (Wien), Gastprof. (FH) Priv.-Doz. Mag. Dr. Wolfgang Weber, MA, MAS (Vorarlberg), Mag. Dr. Florian Wenninger (Wien), Assoz.-Prof.[in] Mag.[a] Dr.[in] Heidrun Zettelbauer (Graz).

Peer-Review Committee (2021–2023):
Ass.-Prof.[in] Mag.[a] Dr.[in] Tina Bahovec (Institut für Geschichte, Universität Klagenfurt), Prof. Dr. Arnd Bauerkämper (Fachbereich Geschichts- und Kulturwissenschaften, Freie Universität Berlin), Günter Bischof, Ph.D. (Center Austria, University of New Orleans), Dr.[in] Regina Fritz (Institut für Zeitgeschichte, Universität Wien/Historisches Institut, Universität Bern), ao. Univ.-Prof.[in] Mag.[a] Dr.[in] Johanna Gehmacher (Institut für Zeitgeschichte, Universität Wien), Univ.-Prof. i. R. Dr. Hanns Haas (Universität Salzburg), Univ.-Prof. i. R. Dr. Ernst Hanisch (Salzburg), Univ.-Prof.[in] Mag.[a] Dr.[in] Gabriella Hauch (Institut für Geschichte, Universität Wien), Univ.-Doz. Dr. Hans Heiss (Institut für Zeitgeschichte, Universität Innsbruck), Robert G. Knight, Ph.D. (Department of Politics, History and International Relations, Loughborough University), Dr.[in] Jill Lewis (University of Wales, Swansea), Prof. Dr. Oto Luthar (Slowenische Akademie der Wissenschaften, Ljubljana), Hon.-Prof. Dr. Wolfgang Neugebauer (Dokumentationsarchiv des Österreichischen Widerstandes, Wien), Mag. Dr. Peter Pirker (Institut für Zeitgeschichte, Universität Innsbruck), Prof. Dr. Markus Reisenleitner (Department of Humanities, York University, Toronto), Dr.[in] Elisabeth Röhrlich (Institut für Geschichte, Universität Wien), ao. Univ.-Prof.[in] Dr.[in] Karin M. Schmidlechner-Lienhart (Institut für Geschichte/Zeitgeschichte, Universität Graz), Univ.-Prof. i. R. Mag. Dr. Friedrich Stadler (Wien), Prof. Dr. Gerald J. Steinacher (University of Nebraska-Lincoln), Assoz.-Prof. DDr. Werner Suppanz (Institut für Geschichte/Zeitgeschichte, Universität Graz), Univ.-Prof. Dr. Philipp Ther, MA (Institut für Osteuropäische Geschichte, Universität Wien), Prof. Dr. Stefan Troebst (Leibniz-Institut für Geschichte und Kultur des östlichen Europa, Universität Leipzig), Prof. Dr. Michael Wildt (Institut für Geschichtswissenschaften, Humboldt-Universität zu Berlin), Dr.[in] Maria Wirth (Institut für Zeitgeschichte, Universität Wien).

zeitgeschichte
49. Jg., Heft 3 (2022)

Migrants and Refugees from the 1960s until Today

Edited by
Wolfgang Mueller and Dirk Rupnow

V&R unipress

Vienna University Press

Contents

Wolfgang Mueller / Dirk Rupnow

Editorial

One of the oldest phenomena in the history of mankind is migration, whether peaceful or violent, voluntary or forced, barely noticeable outflow or mass movements. Although generally a phenomenon of local or regional dimension, at times migration has also occurred at supra-regional or even intercontinental levels. Triggered by climatic changes, hunger and need, conflicts and wars, political persecution, or the pursuit of economic betterment, migration has not only enriched societies and fostered exchange, it has also destabilized nations and caused empires to perish. Some of the most colossal structures on earth – from the *Limes* of the Roman Empire to the Serpent's Wall in Ukraine, from the Great Wall of China to the Iron Curtain – were built to prevent the unwanted movement of people.

In the 19th century, a natural subject of historiographical study was regional migration to frontier territories,[1] as for example in the Russian Empire or the United States of America. In the 1960s there was renewed interest in migration history in Western Europe due to the increase of immigration.[2] With the collapse of the Soviet Union and the so-called Eastern Bloc, the history of borders came again into focus,[3] leading to a new generation in migration history.[4] This development was reinforced by the "migration wave" of 2015.[5]

---

1 V.O. Klyuchevskii, *Kurs Russkoi istorii*, 5 vols., St. Petersburg: Sin. tipografiya 1904–1922; Frederick Jackson Turner, *The Frontier in American History*, New York: Norton 1920.

2 Michael R. Marrus, *The Unwanted: European Refugees in the Twentieth Century*, Oxford: Oxford Univ. Press 1987.

3 Wolfgang Mueller/Libora Oates-Indruchova, Space, Borders, Borderlands: Global and East European Approaches in Historiography, *Österreichische Zeitschrift Für Politikwissenschaft* 42, no. 1 (2013), 43–46.

4 Dirk Hoerder, *Cultures in Contact: World Migrations in the Second Millennium*, Durham: Duke Univ. Press 2002.

5 Jochen Oltmer, *Migration: Geschichte und Zukunft der Gegenwart*, Darmstadt: WBG 2017; Philipp Ther, *Die Außenseiter: Flucht, Flüchtlinge und Integration im modernen Europa*, Berlin: Suhrkamp Verlag 2017; Agnes Bresselau von Bressensdorf, *Über Grenzen: Migration und Flucht in Globaler Perspektive seit 1945*, Göttingen: Vandenhoeck & Ruprecht 2019; Peter

The history of migration to Austria, especially during the Second Republic, has long been a topic overlooked by historians, but received increased attention since the 1980s.[6] In the past decade, the questions of migration remained in the focus, triggered not least by the 50th anniversaries of Austria's three labor recruitment agreements: 1962 with Spain, 1964 with Turkey, and 1966 with Yugoslavia. Accordingly, the "guest worker migration" of the 1960s and early 1970s has been the focus of a number of research projects, as well as exhibitions and retrospectives. Increasingly, research has also shifted to refugees and long-term aspects of migration, in part due to the so-called "long summer of migration" of 2015, but also the refugees who came to Austria in the 1990s as a result of the Yugoslav wars.[7]

The present volume presents research currently being done on the history of migration to or through Austria. Going beyond labor migration, it not only examines migration today, but also the four decades between 1960 and 2000, a period of Austrian contemporary history for which the question of migration has received little attention. Thus, the volume fulfils several desiderata.

Marcel Amoser's contribution examines migration to Austria for purposes of education from the 1960s to the 1980s based on the example of the university town of Innsbruck, a topic related to Amoser's current doctoral thesis project on student protests in Innsbruck from the 1960s to the 1980s. Viktor Ishchenko, Hannes Leidinger and Wolfgang Mueller discuss Jewish emigration from the USSR to Israel via Austria between 1968 and 1990. Maximilian Graf considers Austria as a country of asylum in the 1970s for refugees from the global South. And to conclude, Judith Welz analyzes Austria's asylum system with regard to deportation policies since the early 1990s.

The editors take no responsibility for political statements made by authors quoted in this issue.[8]

Gatrell, *The Unsettling of Europe: The Great Migration, 1945 to the Present*, London: Allen Lane 2019.

6   Eduard Stanek, *Verfolgt Verjagt Vertrieben. Flüchtlinge in Österreich von 1945–1984*, Vienna: Europaverlag 1985; Heinz Fassmann/Rainer Münz, *Einwanderungsland Österreich? Historische Migrationsmuster, aktuelle Trends und politische Maßnahmen*, Vienna: Jugend & Volk 1995; Gernot Heiss/Oliver Rathkolb eds., *Asylland wider Willen: Flüchtlinge in Österreich im europäischen Kontext seit 1914*, Vienna: Jugend & Volk 1995.

7   Börries Kuzmany/Rita Garstenauer eds., *Aufnahmeland Österreich: Über den Umgang mit Massenflucht seit dem 18. Jahrhundert*, Vienna: Mandelbaum 2017.

8   In particular, the editors reject statements made by Nicholas DeGenova claiming that "Israel has no legitimate claim to the heritage of the Holocaust." Quoted in U.S. Commission on Civil Rights, "Campus Anti-Semitism: A Briefing Before the United States Commission on Civil Rights, held in Washington, D.C., November 18, 2005", Briefing Report, Washington, D.C., July 2006, 59.

Articles

Marcel Amoser

Forgotten "Guests": Educational Migration to Austria from the 1960s to the 1980s

I. Introduction[1]

For some years now, migration research in Austria has once again been experiencing a certain boom. This trend was not only stimulated by the fiftieth
anniversaries of the recruitment agreements between Austria and Turkey (2014)
and – to a lesser extent – between Austria and Yugoslavia (2016), but also by the
emotional debates in media and politics about the most recent refugee and
migration movements. The accompanying focus on labor migration and flight
stories in media discourses is undoubtedly of academic and political relevance,
given the long denial, that Austria is an immigration country. Other forms of
migration, however, often remain on the sidelines. If we follow the geographers
Russell King and Parvati Raghuram, this finding applies especially to research on
the educational migration of students.[2] Although student migration is an established object of study in global history research, the topic is still under-
represented in migration studies.[3] This assessment was recently shared by the
historian Isabella Löhr in her analysis of global educational mobility between
1850 and 1930.[4] When contemporary historical studies deal with educational
migration in Austria, they usually do so as part of an institutional history,[5] as a

1 I would like to thank Eric Burton, Tim Corbett, Sylvia Eller, Gerhard Hetfleisch, Benedikt
   Kapferer, Sarah Oberbichler, the editors, and the reviewers for their valuable comments.
2 Russell King/Parvati Raghuram, "International Student Migration. Mapping the Field and New
   Research Agendas," *Population, Space and Place* 19 (2013), 127–137, 128–129.
3 Recent research on international fellowship programs, for example, should be highlighted
   here. Ludovic Tournès/Giles Scott-Smith (eds.), *Global Exchanges. Scholarships and Transnational Circulation in the Modern World* (New York: Berghan Books 2018). The historian
   Hilary Perraton also did central work in her magnum opus on international students since
   the mid-nineteenth century. Hilary Perraton, *International Students 1860–2010. Policy and
   Practice around the World* (Cham 2020: Palgrave Macmillan 2020).
4 Isabella Löhr, *Globale Bildungsmobilität 1850–1930* (Göttingen: Wallstein 2021), 15–17.
5 Michael Dippelreiter, *50 Jahre Bildungsmobilität. Eine kleine Geschichte des ÖAD* (Innsbruck –
   Vienna – Bolzano: StudienVerlag 2011).

secondary topic in a history of development or foreign policy,[6] or as part of a
university or student protest history.[7] This has resulted in important works, but a
systematic examination of educational migration after 1945 in Austria is still a
desideratum.

   This article aims to fill this gap and is dedicated specifically to the history of
student migration to Austria. The aim is to provide an overview of the development of student numbers, countries of origin, and reasons for migration, but
also of the ways in which migration was handled, regulated, and politicized.[8] The
focus lies on the period between the 1960s and 1980s. Educational migration to
Austria reached a peak in the 1960s. Against the backdrop of the decolonization
processes, but also of the Cold War, foreign students[9] took on a special sig-

---

6 Gerald Hödl, *Österreich und die Dritte Welt. Außen- und Entwicklungspolitik der Zweiten
   Republik bis zum EU-Beitritt 1995* (Vienna: Promedia 2004); Eric Burton, "Postkolonialismus,"
   in Marcus Gräser/Dirk Rupnow (eds.), *Österreichische Zeitgeschichte / Zeitgeschichte in Österreich. Eine Standortbestimmung in Zeiten des Umbruchs* (Vienna: Böhlau 2021), 321–347.
7 Ina Friedmann/Dirk Rupnow, *Geschichte der Universität Innsbruck 1669–2019, vol. 1: Phasen
   der Universitätsgeschichte. Partial vol. 2: die Universität im 20. Jahrhundert* (Innsbruck:
   innsbruck university press 2019); Thomas König, *Die Frühgeschichte des Fulbright Program in
   Österreich* (Innsbruck – Vienna – Bolzano: StudienVerlag 2012); on protests by foreign students: Paulus Ebner/Karl Vocelka, *Die zahme Revolution. '68 und was davon blieb* (Vienna:
   Ueberreuter 1998); Fritz Keller, *Wien, Mai 68. Eine heiße Viertelstunde* (Vienna: Mandelbaum
   2008); Oliver Rathkolb/Friedrich Stadler (eds.), *Das Jahr 1968 – Ereignis, Symbol, Chiffre*
   (Göttingen: V&R unipress, 2010).
8 A closer look at the categories of gender and social origin must be reserved for further analyses.
   It can be noted at this point, however, that among foreign students in the mid-1960s, approximately seventeen percent were women. The distribution was country-specific, however,
   as their share among students from so-called developing countries was only half as high.
   Manfred Meyer, *Die ausländischen Studenten in Österreich. Eine soziographische Untersuchung* (Vienna: Ferdinand Berger 1964), 59. As among Austrian students, their proportion
   among foreign students also increased over the years. The Higher Education Report noted a
   noticeable increase from the end of the 1970s onwards and it stood at over thirty percent in the
   following years. With regard to social background, it can be stated that educational migrants
   came predominantly from well-off families, around forty percent having been children from
   academic families, although a comparatively high proportion of working-class children from
   West Germany was also found. Meyer, *ausländische Studenten*, 63–65. Also in the 1970s, it was
   suggested that foreign students came from "upper social classes" to a greater extent than
   Austrian students. *Hochschulbericht 1972*, vol. 1, 78. Parts of this essay are also dealt with in
   more detail in the author's dissertation project on student protests in Innsbruck from the 1960s
   to the 1980s.
9 "Foreign students" here refers to all those students who did not have Austrian citizenship. This
   also corresponds to the use of the category in statistical material after 1945. As always, the use
   of certain categories is accompanied by certain problems. For example, the use of the term
   reproduces a hierarchical differentiation along nationality lines. In a positive sense, however, it
   also names the existing inequalities and historical realities without resorting to euphemisms.
   Furthermore, the connection between educational migration and nationality is unclear. Even
   though they were often congruent in the period under study, not all foreign students had a
   migration experience themselves. In other specific cases, migration for work or flight could
   merge seamlessly.

nificance as part of development policy, which led to the establishment of specialized support services. As a result of the numerus clausus regulation in West Germany and the reforms of Austrian universities in the 1970s, a phase of increased regulation of educational migration set in, which had a detrimental effect on students from certain countries of origin. At the same time, the situation in the largest relevant care institution for foreign students became tense. In 1973/74, the *Österreichischer Auslandsstudentendienst* (Austrian Foreign Student Service, ÖAD) became the subject of student protests that signaled a growing interest in migration policy issues. Finally, in the 1980s a trend towards the internationalization of higher education institutions started to shape the way educational migration is dealt with today.

Reports by *Statistik Austria* (the Austrian Statistical Office), which provide insights into the development of Austrian higher education institutions since 1954, serve as the basis for this paper. In addition, it uses the university reports of the Ministry of Education and Science, which were published at three-year intervals based on a provision in the *Allgemeines Hochschul-Studiengesetz* (General Law on Higher Education, AHStG) of 1966. Furthermore, there are the annual reports of the ÖAD, which, despite the reservation of an idealized self-portrayal, illustrate the activities and problems of the association. Finally, articles from daily newspapers and student magazines as well as ideologically colored leaflets from student groups are analyzed here. Due to the author's research focus on regional history, the materials concentrate on the province of Tyrol. This view from the margins is also pertinent in terms of content: After all, the University of Innsbruck had one of the largest proportions of foreign students in Austria in relation to the total number of students. In the winter semester 1960/61, almost fifty percent of the students in Innsbruck (all student categories)[10] had foreign citizenship. At the University of Vienna, by contrast, the figure was slightly more than 22 percent and thus below the Austrian average of about a quarter of the students.[11] In the winter semester of 1971/72, the proportion of foreign students throughout Austria was around sixteen percent, a quarter of whom were studying in Innsbruck. Altogether, only eleven percent of Austria's student population were enrolled in Innsbruck. Yet in this year, the University of Innsbruck, with almost 2,000 regular foreign students, even surpassed the University of Vienna in absolute numbers (1,830 students).[12] At the beginning of the 1980s, the University

---

10 Students in Austria are divided into three categories during this period: Ordinary students, who meet all the necessary requirements for taking up studies and are enrolled, extraordinary students, who do not yet meet certain criteria but are admitted to supplementary examinations or university courses, and guest listeners, who are already graduates of universities and wish to attend individual courses without taking up further studies.

11 *Hochschulstatistik 1960/61*, 17 and 28.

12 *Hochschulbericht 1972*, vol. 1, 15 and 76.

of Innsbruck had the highest proportion of foreign students (twenty percent), followed by the Montanuniversität Leoben with seventeen percent. Austria-wide, the proportion of foreign students stood at ten percent in 1979/80.[13] In the winter semester of 1989/90, and thus at the end of the period under examination here, the University of Innsbruck still had the largest proportion of foreign students among Austrian universities, at around eighteen percent. At that time, 8.4 percent of all regular students in Austria had foreign citizenship.[14]

II.   Student Numbers and Countries of Origin

Historically, educational migration is not a new phenomenon. It gained importance in the Habsburg Monarchy as early as the mid-nineteenth century as a result of the university reforms initiated under Leopold Count von Thun-Hohenstein. The reforms transformed the universities into modern academic institutions and encouraged migration, for example by making the faculties of philosophy more attractive, by improving the recognition of educational qualifications obtained abroad, and by lifting the ban on studying outside the borders of the empire that the Holy Alliance had previously proclaimed. Nevertheless, migration movements during that time consisted foremost of mobility within the empire to Vienna, making this city one of the most important European university locations of the time.[15] While the two World Wars had a negative impact on student numbers, educational migration once again became an important force after 1945.[16]

However, student numbers recovered only slowly in the first postwar years, reaching a new low point in the mid-1950s due to the low birth rate. In the following years, there was a continuous increase, but the level of the immediate

---

13 *Hochschulbericht 1981*, 139.

14 *Hochschulbericht 1990*, vol. 1, 180–181.

15 Although many of the students came from different parts of the Habsburg Monarchy, they were counted as "foreigners" due to the ethnonational understanding of the state. Löhr, *Globale Bildungsmobilität*, 133–134. In addition to the prestige of the university in the capital, higher pay certainly also motivated the move to Vienna. Jan Surman, "'Peregrinatio Medica.' Mobilität von Medizinern in den Jahren 1848–1914 und die Konstruktion einer Hauptstadtuniversität," in Daniela Angetter/Birgitt Nemec/Herbert Posch/Christiane Druml/Paul Weindling (eds.), *Strukturen und Netzwerke. Medizin und Wissenschaft in Wien 1848–1955* (Göttingen: V&R unipress 2018), 411–424 (650 Jahre Universität Wien – Aufbruch ins neue Jahrhundert 5).

16 *Hochschulbericht 1969*, 16. One exception was migration movements within the Third Reich, which increased temporarily during the Second World War. Overall, the problem for the interpretation and comparability of the figures from this period is that foreign students were not defined according to nationality, but according to the principle of descent. *Hochschulstatistik 1953/54*, 3, 13–14.

postwar years was not reached again until the end of the 1950s.[17] The number of foreign students was also on the rise and the issue of educational migration increasingly attracted political and media attention.[18] The Austrian university statistics for the winter semester of 1958/59 stated that this group had increased so much in recent years that "[...] the question of foreigners studying has become a top-priority problem for Austrian universities. Foreign students form a serious part of the student body in Austria and therefore cannot be neglected wherever higher education issues are discussed."[19] This trend was also evident in the figures. Measured in terms of the total number of students (all student categories), more than one fifth did not have Austrian citizenship in 1955/56, while a few years later it was almost every third student, a high proportion even by international standards. At some universities, the proportion was even higher.[20] In 1955, for example, the South Tyrolean newspaper *Alpenpost* stated that about fifty percent of the students in Innsbruck were foreign citizens and that they would at least prevent the professors from standing before "half-empty lecture halls."[21] Differences were also apparent in different fields of study. In the winter semester of 1957/58, for instance, theology and medicine in Innsbruck and the Faculty of Mechanical and Electrical Engineering at the Graz University of Technology were attended by a majority of foreign nationals. [22]

In 1961/62, more than twice as many students attended Austrian universities than in the mid-1950s. At the same time, a peak of 11,348 foreign students (all student categories) was recorded, which was not to be surpassed until the 1980s.[23] The main countries of origin remained more or less the same over the decades, although they varied according to university location. Apart from Germany, the largest groups were mainly from Greece and Iran. In the 1970s, Italian nationals arrived in increasing numbers, as did Turkish nationals in the 1980s. Traditionally, however, the largest group of foreign students in Austria came from Germany.[24] In the 1960s, they accounted for about thirty percent of all foreign

---

17 *Hochschulbericht 1969*, 14.
18 Meyer, *Die ausländischen Studenten*, 9.
19 *Hochschulstatistik 1958/59*, 27.
20 *Hochschulstatistik 1962/63*, 122; *Hochschulbericht 1969*, 60. Alois Brusatti/Herta Karpstein/ Dieter Wintersberger, *Österreichische Entwicklungshilfe. Leistungen und Möglichkeiten unter besonderer Berücksichtigung der Vermittlung von Wissen und technischem Können* (Vienna: Ferdinand Berger 1963), 34–35.
21 "Beliebt von Persien bis Costa Rica," *Alpenpost*, 7 February 1955, 8.
22 *Hochschulstatistik 1957/58*, 13.
23 *Hochschulstatistik 1962/63*, 122. This was a high number even in international comparison. Austria was thus one of the most popular host countries in 1960, surpassed in absolute numbers only by the USA, France, the FRG, the USSR, and the UK. Perraton, *International Students*, 78.
24 These were mainly students from the FRG, as students from the GDR were not allowed to study abroad in the West for a long time. Meyer, *ausländische Studenten*, 24. The proportion

students in Austria.[25] Educational expansion and the "economic miracle" had already begun in the Federal Republic of Germany (FRG) in the early 1950s. One reason for German migration was probably the country's geographic, linguistic, and historical proximity to Austria. Since many of the German students studied in Innsbruck, the mountains and the associated sporting opportunities were probably also a motive.[26] On the other hand, the so-called *Ausländerstudium* (foreign study) in Austria was little regulated at that time and some universities had the reputation of making low demands on prospective students. Referring to an analysis of the school and university system in Austria from 1965, the historian Thomas König recently pointed out that in German-speaking countries, the Governmental Sciences at the University of Graz in particular had the reputation of having low standards.[27]

In the second half of the 1950s, educational migration from Greece and Hungary was also significant. Those immigrants studied mainly in Vienna, Graz, and Leoben.[28] The migration from Hungary only temporarily took on larger dimensions due to the suppression of the Hungarian uprising in 1956. However, the larger movement from Greece was of a persistent nature. In the winter semester of 1953/54, only 123 Greek students were enrolled at Austrian universities. In 1956/57, this number was already over 1,500. At the beginning of the 1960s, this group made up almost one fifth of the total number of foreign students.[29] Although the numbers declined again in the mid-1960s, Greece was still one of the main countries of origin in the 1980s.[30] According to the university statistics, the reasons for the significant increase in the second half of the 1950s were the political conditions and the introduction of admission restrictions (numerus clausus) in Greece.[31]

It is certainly plausible that the political tensions after the end of the civil war and the nationalist government's repression of alleged or actual political opponents as well as restrictions on university admissions encouraged educational migration. However, these developments are unsatisfactory in explaining why

---

of students who had fled was probably not particularly significant in quantitative terms. However, it was not possible to distinguish between the two German states in the statistics, as most students simply stated "German" as their citizenship. *Hochschulstatistik* 1960/61, 54–55.

25 *Hochschulbericht 1969*, 58; Meyer, *Die ausländischen Studenten*, 24.

26 Meyer, *Die ausländischen Studenten*, 85.

27 Thomas König, "Krise und neue Anforderungen. Das österreichische Hochschulregime 1920–1960 und die Kritik der frühen 1960er-Jahre," *zeitgeschichte* 47 (2020). Special issue: Neue Universitäten. Österreich und Deutschland in den 1960er- und 1970er-Jahren, 15–34, 17.

28 *Hochschulstatistik 1958/59*, 32.

29 *Hochschulstatistik 1953/54*, 24; *Hochschulstatistik 1960/61*, 17–19.

30 *Hochschulstatistik 1965/66*, 40; *Hochschulbericht 1987*, 222.

31 *Hochschulstatistik 1958/59*, 32.

Austria, of all places, was a desired destination.[32] A study published in 1964, which was based on an overall survey of all foreign students and achieved an impressive response rate of over ninety percent, offers further explanations.[33] One frequently cited motivation for studying in Austria was the reputation of the country's universities. This reason might have been convincing for some institutions. However, this reputation was interpreted in exclusively positive terms. As mentioned above, some educational institutions also had a reputation for particularly low standards. Furthermore, social desirability could have contributed to further distortions. The rather unspecific motive of "getting to know the country and its people" could probably be classified in a similar direction. Two other frequently mentioned motives were more substantial: existing social networks and a lack of alternatives. The pragmatic motive that no other university had been found for financial or other reasons even ranked third in the list. It can be deduced from this that Austria was not the desired destination for at least some of the students, but was chosen as a destination to study due to favorable general conditions. The frequent mention of social networks moreover illustrates the relevance of chain migration in the field of university education. In many cases, relatives already lived in Austria, but some also migrated because of recommendations or the influence of Austrian diplomatic missions abroad.[34]

In the case of Greek students, there was a tradition of social, economic, political, and cultural exchange. As an imperial metropole and trading hub, Vienna became a destination for migratory movements from Southeastern Europe during the Habsburg Empire, during which time Greek-Orthodox parishes and a Greek national school were founded.[35] Already in the interwar period, several Greek associations were founded in Vienna, while during the Nazi occupation forced laborers were brought from Greece. In addition, there were some students and collaborators of the Nazi regime, some of whom remained in Austria after the war.[36] The historian Harald Heppner also emphasized with regard to the popular destination Graz that there was a close relationship to Southeastern

---

32 On the political climate of the "ailing democracy" Greece, see: Adamantios T. Skordos, "Die Beziehung Österreichs zur griechischen Junta (1967–1974): Zwischen Verachtung und Pragmatismus," in Stefan A. Müller/ David Schriffl/Adamantios T. Skordos (eds.), *Heimliche Freunde. Die Beziehungen Österreichs zu den Diktaturen Südeuropas nach 1945: Spanien, Portugal, Griechenland* (Vienna – Cologne – Weimar: Böhlau 2016), 235–326, 236–246.

33 Meyer, *Die ausländischen Studenten*, 82–88.

34 Meyer, *Die ausländischen Studenten*, 82–88.

35 Margot Schneider, *Griechische Vereine in Österreich 1918–1974*, unpublished MA thesis, University of Vienna, 2013, 41–42, URL: https://www.byzneo.univie.ac.at/fileadmin/user_u pload/i_byzneo/abschlussarbeiten_stassinopoulou/Diplomarbeit_Schneider_Margot._Griec hische_Vereine_in_OEsterreich_1918-1974.pdf (29 November 2021).

36 Ibid., 36 and 44–51.

Europe at the local university, as reflected in relevant research focuses.[37] Relations were also cultivated – albeit less openly and accompanied by student protests – with the Greek military junta (1967–1974).[38]

At the beginning of the 1960s, Iran became the third most popular country for sending educational migrants to Austria.[39] In the following years, more than 1,000 Iranian students were enrolled at Austrian universities.[40] Due to changes in the requirements for military service and stricter admission requirements at Austrian universities, this number declined at the end of the decade, but Iran remained one of the central countries of origin.[41] After the Islamic Revolution and during the First Gulf War, the number of Iranian students increased again, eventually even exceeding that of the 1960s.[42] Austria also traditionally maintained good relations with Iran. At the end of the 1950s, the country became one of Austria's most important trading partners and thus functioned as a sales market for Austrian products, and was also a market for companies such as VOEST, Böhler, and Elin. Emphasis was also placed on cultural exchange, with the Austrian Cultural Institute in Tehran, founded in 1958, representing a link between the two countries in the domains of culture and science.[43] The oil crisis led to a further intensification of Austrian-Iranian relations.[44] The good relationship between the two states was also evident in the diplomatic and private visits of Shah Mohammad Reza Pahlavi, who had a personal doctor in Vienna.[45] The fact that Austria, like many Western states, had no problem supporting the Shah's dictatorial regime for political and economic reasons was also reflected in the high proportion of development aid in the 1960s. Iran was one of the largest recipients of Austrian development aid in that decade, along with India and

---

37 Harald Heppner, "'Graz und die Griechen' als Beispiel peripherer Kulturrezeption," in Gunnar Hering (ed.), *Dimensionen griechischer Literatur und Geschichte. Festschrift für Pavlos Tzermias zum 65. Geburtstag* (Frankfurt a. M. – Berlin – Bern: Peter Lang 1993), 199–208, 202–206.

38 The foundation of Steyr-Hellas in 1972 was an expression of this relationship. See: Skordos, "Beziehung," 285–296.

39 *Hochschulstatistik 1960/61*, 20.

40 See for example: *Hochschulbericht 1969*, 59.

41 In 1978, there were about 734 regular listeners. However, Iran was still the fourth-largest country of origin. *Universitätsbericht 1978*, 130. On military service in Iran, see: *Rechenschaftsbericht des ÖAD über das Jahr 1968*, 23. It can only be assumed at this point that the new regulation of military service was connected to the high-profile protests of the Iranian opposition abroad.

42 *Hochschulbericht 1984*, 136; in 1987, the number was much higher again, with almost 1,400 students. Iran was the third-largest country of origin at that time. *Hochschulbericht 1987*, 222.

43 Helmut Slaby, *Bindenschild und Sonnenlöwe. Die Geschichte der österreichisch-iranischen Beziehungen bis zur Gegenwart* (Vienna: Verlag der ÖAW 2010), 346–364.

44 Ibid., 364; Hödl, *Österreich*, 144.

45 Slaby, *Bindenschild*, 346–364.

Yugoslavia.[46] Although most of the development aid consisted of export credits, a not insignificant focus was on educational training.[47] This comprised measures in Iran including the establishment of Austrian-Iranian schools or the qualification of specialists – for example in the medical field – but also the training of students in Austria.[48] In addition to these factors and the repressive political climate, the restrictions on admission to Iranian higher education institutions probably also had a favorable effect on the decision to study abroad.[49]

III.   On the Logic of Development Policy

The example of Iran illustrates the relevance of non-European educational migration to Austria, which was increasingly observed from the second half of the 1950s onwards.[50] At the same time, it indicates the importance of students from "developing countries." In 1961/62, about half of the foreign students in Austria came from a "developing country."[51] In addition to the by far largest groups from Greece and Iran, the countries of origin included Egypt, Syria (or the United Arab Republic), Jordan, Iraq, and Turkey. Apart from migration from Egypt, educational migration from the African continent to Austria was quantitatively low.[52]

The listed countries also illustrate the priorities Austria set in its development policy efforts. The fact that it began to engage in development policy must be understood in the context of the conditions of the time: the East-West conflict

---

46 Rudolf Eder/Hermann Krobath, *Die Österreichische Entwicklungshilfe. Politik – Organisation – Leistungen. Handbuch der österreichischen Entwicklungshilfe, Band 2* (Vienna – Dar es Salaam: Forschungsstiftung für Entwicklungshilfe 1972), 206–207.

47 Hödl, *Österreich*, 234–238, 243.

48 Slaby, *Bindenschild*, 342–353.

49 Bahman Nirumand, for example, described the situation in Iran in his autobiography. Bahman Nirumand, *Weit entfernt von dem Ort, an dem ich sein müsste. Autobiographie* (Hamburg: Rowohlt 2011).

50 Meyer, *Die ausländischen Studenten*, 9.

51 Brusatti, *Österreichische Entwicklungshilfe*, 34. The OECD classification was used, but definitions could vary. In addition to per capita income and various production factors, recipient countries of development aid loans according to the allocation guidelines of the Bretton Woods institutions were also used as a basis for classification. Meyer, *Die ausländischen Studenten*, 25.

52 In 1960/61, for example, 688 regular students came from Africa, 655 of them from Egypt. *Hochschulstatistik 1960/61*, 19; in 1971/72 there were 180 regular students, 129 of them from Egypt. *Hochschulbericht 1972*, vol. 1, 75–76. The numbers increased in the following years. In 1987 there were 583 regular students, 251 of them from Egypt. *Hochschulbericht 1987*, vol. 2, 555. The high number of Egyptian students still reaching into the 1960s is possibly related to the Suez Crisis and Gamal Abdel Nasser's pan-Arab as well as anticolonial sense of mission, which shaped Egypt's migration policy at that time. See on this: Gerasimos Tsourapas, *The Politics of Migration in Modern Egypt. Strategies for Regime Survival in Autocracies* (Cambridge: Cambridge University Press 2019), 59–89.

and decolonization. In the 1950s and 1960s, numerous new states gained independence.[53] Due to the ideological and political tensions between the two superpowers, the young independent states increasingly became the focus of geostrategic considerations, especially after the conferences in Bandung (1955) and Belgrade (1961) and the formation of the Non-Aligned Movement. Both the USSR and the USA – among many other states – tried to gain influence in these countries with the help of development aid programs. In the 1950s and 1960s, special emphasis was therefore put on the education of students from the "Third World."[54]

After joining the OECD, Austria committed itself to provide development aid in the early 1960s. Precisely because of its official neutrality and simultaneous orientation towards the West, the idea was widespread that the country had a special foreign policy role to play in creating trust in former colonies and introducing them to the economic and value system of the West. One common assumption was that Austria was also predestined for this task because of its colonial integrity.[55] In a study on Austrian development aid published in 1963 – with the participation of the economic and social historian Alois Brusatti – this was even seen as a main reason for the migration movements to Austria.[56] That this account was without empirical evidence and rather provided insight into how academic and political elites wanted to see themselves internationally at the time was made clear by another study published a short time later. This overall survey of foreign students found that neither political reasons in general nor the "Myth of Colonial Immaculacy"[57] were relevant when it came to motivations for studying in Austria.[58]

Analogous to the idea of "guest work," the residence of foreign students was only intended to be temporary. After their return migration, they were to contribute to the building of their countries as a future elite, remembering the positive time they had spent in Austria. Bruno Kreisky shared this instrumental view. During his time as Foreign Minister, he emphasized the strategic im-

53 Rossen Djagalov/Christine Evans, "Moscow, 1960: How Soviet Friendship with the 3rd World was Imagined", in Andreas Hilger (ed.), *Die Sowjetunion und die Dritte Welt. UdSSR, Staatssozialismus und Antikolonialismus im Kalten Krieg 1945–1991* (Munich: De Gruyter 2009), 83–105, 84–88.

54 Constantin Katsakioris, "The Lumumba University in Moscow: Higher education for a Soviet-Third-World alliance, 1960–91," *Journal of Global History* 14 (2019) 2, 281–300, 282.

55 Hödl, *Österreich*, 68–80 and 199–200.

56 Brusatti, *Österreichische Entwicklungshilfe*, 35.

57 Clemens Pfeffer, "Koloniale Fantasien Made in Austria. Koloniale Afrikarepräsentationen im österreichischen Nationalrat am Wendepunkt zum Postkolonialismus 1955–1965," in Manuel Menrath (ed.), *Afrika im Blick. Afrikabilder im deutschsprachigen Europa 1870–1970* (Zurich: Chronos 2012), 99–122, 103.

58 Meyer, *Die ausländischen Studenten*, 82–88.

portance of development aid for the victory of the Western system in the "polarization process" in a speech at the Europe Talks on 23 June 1962. Educating students from developing countries in Austria would help "to lead their peoples out of a-historicity," but also ensure that they "remain attached to Austrian culture and to the economic life of our country and will still render us valuable services in the future."[59] This argumentation was probably influenced by the near-escalation of the East-West conflict at Checkpoint Charlie in October 1961, but it also provides insight into Austria's political and economic self-interests that accompanied its commitment to development policy.

Sufficient support services and good study conditions as well as a discrimination-free everyday life were highlighted to illustrate Austria's "hospitality." At the same time, there was a general expectation that the so-called "right of hospitality" should not be abused through ingratitude or even political activity.[60] Such ideas also found their way into media discourses. In the *Tiroler Tageszeitung* – the daily with the largest circulation in Tyrol – criticism of widespread discrimination was voiced by a journalist at the beginning of the 1960s. Social isolation, prejudices, and inflated room rates would ultimately damage Austria's reputation. Foreign students were considered representatives of their countries and negative experiences thus had far-reaching consequences: "The image they take with them here of our European culture and the Occident determines the attitude of their countries towards Europe."[61] In the logic of the East-West conflict and the fear of decolonization, it was further argued that a lack of "hospitality" had led people like Jomo Kenyatta, Ho Chi Minh, and also leading heads of Red China to turn to communism.[62] Given the high number of foreign students in the early 1960s and their strategic importance, it is not surprising that they became the subject of increased regulation and attention in the following years.

---

59 Bruno Kreisky, "Die Rolle Österreichs im Rahmen der Entwicklungshilfe Europas, Europagespräch, Wien 23. Juni 1962," in *Kreisky Reden*, vol. 1 (Vienna: Österreichische Staatsdruckerei 1981), 350–359, 351 and 356–357.
60 In the case of political activities, critics repeatedly spoke of an "abuse of the right to hospitality," for example in connection with the politicization at the beginning of the 1960s: *Der Innsbrucker Student* 4 (June 1963), 4.
61 "Studierende aus fünf Erdteilen in Innsbruck," *Tiroler Tageszeitung*, 27 April 1960, 3.
62 Ibid., 3.

IV. Educational Migration as an Object of Regulation and Attention

The increase in the total number of students at the beginning of the 1960s revealed structural problems in the Austrian university system such as chronic underfunding as well as personnel and infrastructural bottlenecks. As a result of economic boom and educational expansion, the *Ordinarienuniversität*, which had been restored by the *Hochschul-Organisationsgesetz* (Law on the Organization of Higher Education) of 1955, was confronted with demands that required, on the one hand, a rationalization of university education in the sense of a faster "production" of academics for the labor market and, on the other hand, a more efficient design of the educational content in line with technological innovations. However, the education budget lagged behind these ambitions.[63]

In the area of responsibility of the *Österreichische Volkspartei* (Austrian People's Party, ÖVP) – which formed a unitary government in 1966 – a forward-looking education policy began in the mid-1960s, which brought about infrastructural expansions, budget increases, and the institutionalization of educational research. It also meant a changed approach to foreign students. Initially, some fields of study were devoted to the situation of foreign students, especially from so-called developing countries.[64] Catching up on knowledge production was accompanied by regulations. In particular, the varying level of proficiency in German posed problems for the universities. At the University of Innsbruck, a compulsory German examination was therefore introduced as early as 1962.[65] Other universities also adopted similar measures within their autonomous sphere of influence.[66] To acquire the necessary qualifications, language courses and, from 1962/63, pre-study programs were set up. These measures established new hurdles with critical consequences: While the number of extraordinary students increased, the number of educational migrants decreased, levelling off at around 9,000 in 1963/64.[67] The General Law on Higher Education (AHStG) of 1966 was also a sign of regulation, creating a legal basis for the admission of foreign students based on an equivalence assessment, the availability of places,

63 Wolf Frühauf, "Einleitung zu Hertha Firnberg. Die Wissenschaft in der modernen Welt," in Hubert Christian Ehalt/Oliver Rathkolb (eds.), *Wissens- und Universitätsstadt Wien. Eine Entwicklungsgeschichte seit 1945* (Göttingen: V&R unipress 2015), 107–112, 107.

64 From 1963 onwards, the ÖAD Research Institute published the series "Österreichische Schriften zur Entwicklungshilfe."

65 Protocol of the Academic Senate of the University of Innsbruck, 25 October 1962. Senate meeting minutes. University Archive Innsbruck.

66 Meyer, *Die ausländischen Studenten*, 60.

67 *Hochschulbericht 1969*, 60; Meyer, *Die ausländischen Studenten*, 60.

and a performance-oriented ranking of applicants.[68] If equivalence was not determined by the rectorate or a subordinate body, supplementary examinations, university courses, and language courses could henceforth be demanded by law.[69] Aside from that part of the student population for whom special provisions existed on the basis of bilateral agreements, the AHStG thus brought with it significant hurdles.[70] Despite Austria-wide standardization, however, the law offered a great deal of room for interpretation, which led to different implementations at the individual university locations.

In addition to the regulation of access to higher education, the need for support institutions also became apparent with the increase in foreign students. Among the institutions founded at this time were the *Hammer-Purgstall-Gesellschaft* (Hammer-Purgstall Society, 1958), the *Afro-Asiatisches-Institut* (Afro-Asian Institute, 1959), the *Österreichischer Auslandsstudentendienst* (Austrian Foreign Student Service, 1961) and the *Österreichische Lateinamerika-Institut* (Austrian Latin America Institute, 1965). For a larger proportion of foreign students, the ÖAD, which had been initiated by the *Österreichische Rektorenkonferenz* (Austrian Rectors' Conference) and the *Österreichische Hochschülerschaft* (Austrian Student Union, ÖH), was of particular importance. The offices in the individual university towns provided information on questions about studies, scholarships, and residence requirements and arranged rooms and work. The ÖAD also had its own publications, *Nota Bene* and *Briefe aus Österreich* (Letters from Austria), which informed foreign students about life in Austria and were intended to promote a positive image of the country. An information and documentation center also served as a networking forum with various development aid institutions. From 1963 until its fusion with the *Afro-Asiatisches-Institut* in 1966/67, it published a series of studies devoted to various facets of educational migration to Austria. From 1962, the ÖAD also took over the disbursement of scholarships, but only relatively few students came to Austria through such programs – the majority of foreign students were financed by their families.[71]

The ÖAD was not only a support structure but also exercised a controlling function. Against the background of the student movement and its aftermath, this repeatedly led to conflicts that came to a head in the mid-1970s. At that time, the university was already characterized by a restrictive attitude towards foreign students.

---

68 *AHStG* 1966 §7 (6), RIS, https://www.ris.bka.gv.at/Dokumente/BgblPdf/1966_177_0/1966_1 77_0.pdf (19 November 2021).
69 Ibid., §7 (7–10).
70 Ibid., §7 (11).
71 Dippelreiter, *50 Jahre*, 24–25 and 30–33; Meyer, *Die ausländischen Studenten*, 65.

V.   Semi-Opened Universities: Educational Migration in the 1970s

In the 1970s, the number of students increased significantly – especially with the fall of tuition fees. In 1969/70, less than 41,000 Austrian students were enrolled, this number increasing to almost 59,000 in 1973/74.[72] However, the expansion of the (Austrian) student quota pushed by the *Sozialdemokratische Partei Öster-reichs* (Social Democratic Party of Austria, SPÖ) with its guiding principles "education for all" and "education is a human right" relied on a national mindset and paradoxically aggravated the situation for foreign students in Austria. Opening and democratizing the universities can therefore only be understood as modernization by halves. This was already made clear by the *Hochschul-Taxen-gesetz* (Law on Higher Education Fees) of 1972, which differentiated by nation-ality. Those foreign students who were not exempted from paying tuition fees because of existing bilateral agreements or because they came from a "developing country" still had to pay fees.[73] Inequalities also became apparent in the reform of the *Hochschülerschaftsgesetz* (Student Union Law) in 1973. Until then, the ÖH had only been defined as an association of Austrian students, which meant that large sections of students were also excluded from the right to vote. This was increasingly problematized by the student movement, especially because the exclusion of foreign students in the ÖH was a weak point for general demands for co-determination. An expansion of political participation opportunities there-fore received the support of most student factions of the time.[74] However, the question of passive voting rights became a central bone of contention between progressive student representatives, academic senates, and the Rectors' Con-ference.[75] The exaggerated fear that foreign students could influence Austrian legislation and perhaps even lead to communist infiltration caused critics of full voting rights to raise concerns. In addition, there was the anxiety of a retroactive effect on the redrafting of the *Arbeitsverfassungsgesetz* (Labor Constitution Law). A passive ÖH right to vote could therefore have served as a basis for argu-mentation to implement such a right for work council elections as well. Finally,

---

72 *Hochschulbericht 1975*, 26.

73 *Hochschul-Taxengesetz* § 10 u. 11, RIS, https://www.ris.bka.gv.at/Dokumente/BgblPdf/1972
    _76_0/1972_76_0.pdf (30 November 2021).

74 Michael Ruß, "Demokratisierung der Hochschule ohne Ausländer?," *Signum* 4 (July 1968), 7–
    11, 7; Letter from the Austrian Student Union to the Presidium of the National Council
    "Begutachtung Hochschülerschaftsgesetz-Novelle," 7 May 1995, Republic of Austria. Par-
    liament, https://www.parlament.gv.at/PAKT/VHG/XIX/SNME/SNME_00325/imfname_446
    070.pdf (23 November 2021).

75 For example: Protocol of the Academic Senate of the University of Innsbruck, 29 October
    1970, 8. Senate Meeting Minutes. Innsbruck University Archives; "Vernichtende Kritik am
    ÖH-Gesetzentwurf," *Unipress* 3 (WS 1972/73), 2.

resistance from employee representatives ensured that the new ÖH law only provided for active voting rights for foreign nationals.[76] The democratization of the university thus made decisive progress, but the extent to which it was realized varied along passport lines.

Unequal treatment and hierarchies shaped by the nation state were also evident in the regulation of so-called studies for foreigners. The Higher Education Report of 1972 already stated that the increased enrolment of Austrian students would have a negative effect on the availability of university places for foreign nationals.[77] However, restrictions on admission in other European countries were particularly significant for the debate on limiting the number of foreign students. The numerus clausus introduced in West Germany in 1968 led to a steep increase of student numbers in certain fields of study. With the traditionally highest proportion of West German students, the University of Innsbruck came under particular pressure. In the winter semester of 1972/73 alone, there were about 3,000 applicants from West Germany.[78] The situation preoccupied universities, the Rectors' Conference, and the Ministry of Science in the mid-1970s. The result was a more restrictive interpretation of the existing law.[79] In addition to a strict handling of the "equivalence clause," affecting the recognition of qualifications acquired abroad and possible allocation to pre-study programs, "maximum quotas" for foreign students were introduced for certain subjects. From 1973/74 onwards, the Academic Senate determined each semester which courses at the university were to be open, partially accessible, or completely closed to foreign students. The heavily regulated subjects included medicine and psychology as well as biology, chemistry, geography, and architecture.[80] In addition, the Rectors' Conference set up a "Committee for the Assessment of Foreign Matriculation Certificates" in the summer semester of 1974. This committee drew up a paper on the "Admission Requirements for Foreign Applicants to Austrian Universities of Applied Sciences" which formed the basis for "recommendations" by the Rectors' Conference. Although this was not a legally binding regulation, the rectors agreed to take the paper into account as an "implementation guideline." At the same time, this was supposed to lead to an Austria-wide "harmonization" in dealing with foreign students, who had been treated differently due to different interpretations of the existing legal situation

---

76 "Profil über ÖH-Wahlen," in *Unipress* 4 (WS 1973/74), 14; "AK-Stellungnahme," *Unipress* 3 (WS 1972/73), 3. On the link between the ÖH Law and the Labor Constitution Law, see also: "Arbeiterkammer: Um das Wahlrecht für Ausländer," *Tiroler Tageszeitung*, 24 April 1973, 2.

77 *Hochschulbericht 1972*, 74–75.

78 *Hochschulbericht 1972*, 261; *Hochschulbericht 1975*, 38.

79 *Hochschulbericht 1978*, 24.

80 *Hochschulbericht 1974*, 38.

at the individual university locations.[81] Probably the most far-reaching instrument of the recommendation in this context was that of a "remote effect of the numerus clausus." The recommendations stated: "Foreign university entrants who are admitted in their home country only based on an additional entrance examination or on the basis of successfully completed further preliminary studies must prove that they have passed the required preliminary examinations and have been admitted to the program."[82]

This meant that – provided there were no special intergovernmental solutions – foreign students in Austria were subject to the admission requirements of the planned degree program in their home countries. This regulation not only had consequences for the intended target group of West German students, but also for Iranian and Greek students who could not take up university studies in their home countries for political reasons. The regulation therefore also quickly evoked protests from left-wing groups, which had a certain popularity in the aftermath of the student movement at universities in the 1970s. For the electoral platform *Offensiv Links* (Offensively Left) – an alliance of the *Zentrum Basisdemokratischer Sozialisten* (Center for Grassroots Democratic Socialists) in Innsbruck and the Vienna University group of the *Freie Österreichische Jugend. Bewegung für Sozialismus* (Free Austrian Youth: Movement for Socialism) – these represented disadvantages for an already vulnerable group. They also saw it as the harbinger of a numerus clausus for all.[83] Activists of the *Kommunistische Gruppe Innsbruck* (Innsbruck Communist Group), who were committed to a dogmatic form of Marxism-Leninism, argued similarly. In their view, the exclusion of foreign colleagues was an expression of a general crisis of imperialism and a diversionary maneuver of the bourgeoisie, which used division to divert attention from capitalism as the real cause of the problem. In this way, the university measures were at the same time linked to the situation of migrant workers in Austria, who were increasingly confronted with dismissals and xenophobic resentment during the oil crisis.[84]

---

81 "Empfehlungen der Österreichischen Rektorenkonferenz. Zulassungsbedingungen für ausländische Studienbewerber an den österreichischen Hochschulen" – erstellt vom 'Ausschuß zur Beurteilung ausländischer Reifezeugnisse,' *Rechenschaftsbericht des ÖAD über das Jahr 1974*, 67–68.

82 Even if a student had passed the entrance examination in his or her home country, he or she still had to have an excellent school leaving certificate. In this context, a conversion scheme of grading scales was developed for individual countries, which was to serve as an orientation throughout Austria. "Empfehlungen," 68.

83 Offensiv Links, "Wir kandidieren," 1975, 10. Private archive of Volker Schönwiese (original in possession of the author).

84 Elisabeth Senn, "Numerus Clausus für Ausländer!," 1974/75. Collection of leaflets. University Archive Innsbruck.

The new measures resulted in a decline in applications from abroad.[85] The effects were most evident in the first-time enrolments of students from West Germany. In 1974/75, only half as many first-time enrolments came from the FRG compared to 1970/71. By contrast, between 1970/71 and 1974/75, the number of first-time enrolments from Italy (especially South Tyrol) doubled, almost equaling those of West German students.[86] The improved economic and social situation in South Tyrol probably played a role here, which had a beneficial effect on the expansion of education. With the Second Statute of Autonomy in 1972, which transferred central competences – for example in the area of education – from the Italian state to South Tyrol, as well as the successive implementation of ethnic proportional representation in the allocation of public positions, the perspectives for qualified German-speaking personnel increased.[87] The lack of a local university in South Tyrol as well as the spatial and, for part of the population, linguistic and historical proximity to Austria probably encouraged the decision to migrate to Austria, with Innsbruck being one of the most popular destinations. This migration was also fostered by a bilateral agreement in 1972 that facilitated access to higher education and expanded existing arrangements.[88] Although students from the FRG remained the largest group of educational migrants in Austria, the gap to Italian citizens became increasingly smaller. Whereas in the winter semester of 1971/72, around 29 percent of the foreign regular students were from West Germany and around 10 percent from Italy, in 1974/75 there were 25 percent from the FRG and 19 percent from Italy.[89]

There were also significant shifts in the first-time enrolment of foreign nationals for the study of medicine. Due to particularly high demand, some universities began to regulate this subject as early as the end of the 1960s. The number of almost 500 first-time enrolments in 1968/69 fell continuously in the following years and in 1974/75 comprised only 141 persons throughout Austria.[90] The number of foreign students in philosophy as well as economic and social science courses increased at the same time.[91] This may indicate that less regulated

---

85 "Empfehlung der Österreichischen Rektorenkonferenz. Zulassungsbedingungen für ausländische Studienbewerber an den österreichischen Universitäten – erstellt vom Ausschuss zur Beurteilung ausländischer Reifezeugnisse (beschlossen von der Österreichischen Rektorenkonferenz am 30. Juni 1975)," *Rechenschaftsbericht des ÖAD über das Jahr 1975*, 53.
86 *Hochschulbericht 1975*, 38.
87 Rolf Steininger, *Südtirol. Vom Ersten Weltkrieg bis zur Gegenwart* (Innsbruck – Vienna: Haymon 2015⁴), 162–168.
88 *Hochschulbericht 1978*, 24.
89 *Hochschulbericht 1972*, 75–76; *Hochschulbericht 1975*, 35. This ratio remained more or less the same from the mid-1970s until the end of the 1980s. In 1989/90, the two groups were evenly matched, each with around a quarter of foreign students. *Hochschulbericht 1990*, 182.
90 *Hochschulbericht 1975*, 37. On the regulations of the Medical Faculty of the University of Vienna at the end of the 1960s, see: *Rechenschaftsbericht des ÖAD über das Jahr 1968*, 23.
91 *Hochschulbericht 1975*, 36.

subjects acted as a fallback solution to undertake studies in Austria despite the restrictions. Such shifts, but also new bilateral agreements with exemption provisions, had the effect that the number of foreign students remained constant at around 9,300 persons (all student categories).[92] However, their share in the total number of students declined due to the continued and strong growth of Austrian students.

VI.   The ÖAD Challenged

During the regulation phase, there was increasing tension in the ÖAD. As early as autumn 1970, participants in the pre-study program in Mödling[93] protested, and in the following years, too, the often seemingly arbitrary assignments in the courses, but also the curricula and the examinations were the subject of criticism. The Ministry of Science reacted by setting up its own commission to analyze accusations and develop solutions. In addition, a study was commissioned that dealt with the social effects of the spatial segregation of the Mödling pre-study program from a psychological perspective, but it remained without further political consequences.[94] The lines of conflict therefore led to further protests in 1973/74. The anti-ÖAD protests – including rallies, signature campaigns, strikes, teach-ins, and leafleting – were mainly addressed to two institutions of the association. First, the pre-study programs were criticized for their compulsory nature, as those affected lost several semesters before their desired course of study could be taken up. Problems also existed in determining the equivalence of foreign school-leaving certificates. In a study commissioned by the Ministry of Science in response to the protests in 1974, the educationalist Walter Berger identified an unequal treatment of students from so-called "developing countries." Even though similar educational systems had been installed in those countries because of colonialism as in the countries of their former colonizers, students from the former had to enter the pre-study program while students from the latter were usually allowed to study immediately – provided there were no further admission restrictions.[95] The content design also met with criticism. Instead of focusing only on learning the German language, other subjects had to

---

92 Ibid., 35.
93 In 1962, in a secluded boarding school in Mödling and under the direction of the ÖAD, the first pre-study course was established to prepare foreign students for studies at an Austrian university. Dippelreiter, *50 Jahre*, 26 and 29.
94 Dippelreiter, *50 Jahre*, 47–49; *Hochschulbericht 1972*, vol. 1, 79.
95 Berger, *Die Eingliederung nichtdeutschsprachiger Ausländer in die österreichischen Hochschulen. Alternativen zum Vorstudienlehrgang* (Munich: Jugend und Volk, 1974), 11 and 18–21.

be completed, some of which were not relevant to the studies or the knowledge had already been acquired in the home country anyway. The subject of European Studies met with particular resistance, as it was perceived primarily as a forum for Austria's self-promotion and the superiority of the Western system. In a polemical tone, Walter Berger stated:

> "It is all too easy for the suspicion to grow that the Europeanizing superimpositions on national education are aimed at raising a privileged class that is alienated from its own people and that obeys Europe. Allusions to 'manipulation' in the sense of a hidden cultural imperialism accumulated in pamphlets by discontented groups of foreigners and began to take root in people's minds."[96]

Walter Berger led the pre-study program in Mödling between 1962 and 1964 and therefore had an inside view for his analysis. Although the study partly reads like a personally motivated reckoning with the ÖAD, given the sometimes pointed style and argumentation, he got to the heart of the widespread discontent.

Even more drastic was the criticism of the so-called lecturers of confidence, who were appointed from the pool of academic staff. This position, introduced in 1963, was supposed to provide foreign students with a specific contact person for university-related as well as social or cultural problems. Due to their far-reaching competences and lack of control, however, they fulfilled an ambivalent function. For example, agreements existed between the ÖAD, the regional employment offices, and the police that made the possibility of taking up employment as well as the issuing or extension of residence permits dependent on the decision of the lecturers of confidence. Some supervisors criticized the resulting additional workload, but at the same time saw an opportunity to improve the often only loose contact with foreign students.[97] First and foremost, decisions were supposed to be based on the academic success of the person being supervised, but in some cases other criteria played a role. The Innsbruck lecturer of confidence Osmund Menghin – son of the prehistorian Oswald Menghin[98] – also saw this as a means of "checking [...] behavior on academic soil."[99] Against the background of the student protests and the Six-Day War, it is not unlikely that the agreement with the police introduced in 1967 was also understood as a political instrument of control. After all, the Ministry of the Interior had made it clear in the news-

---

96 Berger, *Eingliederung*, 28.
97 *Rechenschaftsbericht des ÖAD über das Jahr 1969*, 46.
98 Oswald Menghin was a prehistorian and rector of the University of Vienna in 1935/36. In the Seyß-Inquart Anschluss Cabinet, he was responsible for the implementation of the Nuremberg Race Laws in the field of education. Otto H. Urban, "Oswald Menghin. Professor für Urgeschichte, Unterrichtsminister 1938," in Mitchell Ash/Josef Ehmer (eds.), *Universität – Politik – Gesellschaft* (Göttingen: V&R unipress 2015), 299–304 (650 Jahre Universität Wien – Aufbruch ins neue Jahrhundert 2).
99 *Rechenschaftsbericht des ÖAD über das Jahr 1967*, 48.

paper *Nota Bene* in 1966 that for them "'quasi-students' represent a danger to the maintenance of public security."[100] In addition, supervisors had contact with embassies of other countries. This was delicate in the case of the dictatorships in Iran and Greece and the conflicts between critics and supporters of the regimes in Austria.[101]

A meeting of the Academic Senate in Innsbruck in 1967 illustrates that this extensive concentration of power was also criticized in part by the academic staff. Rudolf Bratschitsch, who later became rector, questioned whether it was "legally justifiable" that foreign students had to ask for a recommendation from the lecturers of confidence before they were granted or received an extension on a residence permit.[102] Despite such objections, the Ministry of the Interior only revoked the agreement by decree in 1974, as it was then no longer considered "necessary."[103] The protests against the ÖAD in 1973/74 played an important role in this. In May 1973, the situation in Mödling initially caused criticism again, which even led to small successes. This is partly because, following the ÖH reform, the student body now also participated and because Austrian dailies and the *Österreichischer Rundfunk* (Austrian Broadcasting Corporation, ORF) also took an interest in the protests. To ease the situation, the ÖAD moved the pre-studies program to Ottakring, but the protests continued in the following year. Influenced by the agitation of left-wing student groups, foreign students of the pre-studies program went on strike and demanded the abolition of the ÖAD, the pre-study program, and the system of the lecturers of confidence. The protests reached their climax on 19 March 1974 with the temporary occupation of the ÖAD office in Vienna. The media echo of this action, the extension of the strike activities to Graz and Innsbruck, and the ÖH's withdrawal from the ÖAD, commented with a polemical public letter, made clear the urgent need for action. The evaluation in the form of Walter Berger's study was finally followed by a reform of the ÖAD: The competences of the confidential lecturers were re-stricted, the pre-study programs were temporarily no longer carried out via the ÖAD and were now non-binding, and European Studies was finally dropped.[104]

100 "Betreuung," *Nota Bene* (September 1966), 27.
101 Dippelreiter, *50 Jahre*, 36–37.
102 Protocol of the Academic Senate of the University of Innsbruck, 27 April 1967, 15. Senate Meeting Minutes. University Archive Innsbruck.
103 *Rechenschaftsbericht des ÖAD über das Jahr 1975*, 39.
104 *Hochschulbericht 1975*, 38; Dippelreiter, *50 Jahre*, 52–60.

VII. Internationalization as an Agenda

While it became increasingly difficult for students from certain countries to take up studies in Austria, an internationalization boost began in the 1980s. Indicators of this were the increase in inter-state and inter-university partnership agreements. The early agreements with Finland (1969), Italy (1972), and Luxembourg (1972) were joined in the later 1970s by agreements with Bulgaria (1976), Yugoslavia (1976), and Liechtenstein (1977).[105] By 1987, cultural and exchange agreements existed with 31 other states.[106] A similar trend can be observed with regard to the development of partnership agreements between individual Austrian and foreign universities. While only five such agreements existed by 1975, by 1987 there were already forty.[107] This development also reflects the attitude of the Austrian Rectors' Conference, which included the "internationality of universities" as a priority in its 1981 work program.[108]

The international cooperation network created a system of exemptions that – depending on the specific wording of the agreements – counteracted the existing restrictions on admission. It is therefore not surprising that the number of foreign students rose again. In the winter semester of 1983/84, the earlier peak number of foreign students (all student categories) of 1961/62 was exceeded with 13,442 persons. However, the increase in the number of Austrian students continued to be much stronger, which is why the relative share of foreign students – with a downward trend – was 9.5 percent.[109] In addition to the special agreements, however, a revision of the implementation guidelines of the Rectors' Conference in the 1980s also had an impact on the presence of educational migrants at universities. As a result of the amendment of the AHStG, the National Council passed a formal resolution in 1982 requesting greater consideration of "development policy aspects" in the allocation of study places. Starting in the winter semester of 1982/83, students from "developing countries" were given preferential treatment in restricted study programs. In addition, the "remote effect of the numerus clausus" did not apply if direct university access in the home country was denied for "unavoidable reasons."[110] This meant that Austrian universities were reopened to applicants who had been refused a place at university for political reasons. Students from Iran, for example, who were confronted with the Gulf War and the consequences of the Islamic Revolution, benefited from this, as did students from Turkey, who in the 1980s became the

---

105 *Hochschulbericht 1978*, 24.
106 *Hochschulbericht 1987*, vol. 1, 404.
107 *Hochschulbericht 1987*, vol. 1, 405–406.
108 *Hochschulbericht 1981*, 36.
109 *Hochschulbericht 1984*, 133.
110 *Rechenschaftsbericht des ÖAD über das Jahr 1982*, 76–79.

fourth-largest foreign student group after West Germany, Italy, and Iran.[111] In the wake of the military coup in Turkey in 1980, growing numbers of refugees came to Austria. After all, numerous people had already migrated to Austria for work since the 1960s. Family and friendship networks existed that could influence the choice of where to study. Despite the structural barriers of the Austrian education system, the first children of Turkish labor migrants who had come through family reunification or had already been born in Austria but had Turkish citizenship probably also enrolled in the 1980s. They also benefited from the 1981 amendment to the AHStG through facilitated access to higher education, provided they could prove that they had an Austrian secondary school leaving certificate or if one of their parents had an Austrian passport.[112]

As the 1981 University Report made clear, this amendment also reflected the discussion on accession to the European Economic Community and Austria's growing international networking: "The reformulation of the provisions on the admission of foreigners serves above all to adapt to conditions in Europe. It also takes into account the fact that Austria is the seat of international organizations."[113] This logic was also followed by the treatment of certain groups on equal standing with Austrian nationals. Among them were members of diplomatic missions, consulates, as well as international organizations and journalists from abroad.[114]

Austria's participation in various international conferences was also marked by the Europeanization of the field of higher education. In 1981, for example, the Austrian municipality of Laxenburg became the venue for an EEC event on "Academic Mobility in Europe." In 1984, the Rectors' Conference, the Ministry of Science and the Federal Chamber of Commerce organized a conference on the "Internationality of Austrian Universities in Teaching and Research." The result was a catalogue of measures that flowed into the drafting of another amendment to the AHStG.[115] From 1989 onwards, this facilitated cooperation between Austrian and foreign universities and participation in international study programs. Innovations also became apparent in teaching. A legal framework was henceforth in place to hold courses or entire degree programs in a foreign language – this had previously been reserved for specific degree programs. In addition, papers could be written in a foreign language, provided the assessor agreed. The amendment also brought innovations with regard to the international recognition of Austrian

---

111 *Hochschulbericht 1981*, 141; *Hochschulbericht 1984*, 136.
112 *Hochschulbericht 1981*, 138–139; *Amendment AHStG 1981* §7 (11), RIS, https://www.ris.bk a.gv.at/Dokumente/BgblPdf/1981_332_0/1981_332_0.pdf (30 November 2021).
113 *Hochschulbericht 1981*, 139.
114 Ibid., 138f.; *AHStG 1981* §7 (11).
115 *Hochschulbericht 1984*, 238.

educational qualifications. Certificates could now also be issued in a non-German language.[116]

A push toward internationalization was also expressed in the participation of Austrian universities in international programs and institutions. This included participation in various projects of the European Cooperation in Science and Technology (COST) as well as memberships in the intergovernmental organization for research and development EUREKA, founded in 1985 and in the European Space Agency (ESA).[117] The ERASMUS program, which was initiated in 1987, was of particular importance for educational migration within Europe. Austria sought access to the ERASMUS program as early as the late 1980s within the framework of its EFTA membership, and in 1992/93 it participated for the first time with hundreds of students. To promote the traditionally rather low interest in stays abroad in Austria, the existing scholarship network was also further expanded.[118]

Internationalization changed the overall framework for educational migration – at least for students from certain countries. This was also accompanied by a shift in common perspective. While foreign students were still primarily associated with development policy and "numerus clausus refugees" in the 1970s, they now increasingly became a resource in the international competition between locations. According to the social scientist Martin Winter, the first phase of the *Verwettbewerblichung* (growing competition) between universities began in the 1980s: "Competition was to be for resources in the broadest sense, especially for third-party funding, prizes, academic staff, students, and for positions in all kinds of performance comparisons."[119] The extension of the principle of free-market competition to educational institutions not only shaped their relationships with each other, but also resulted in far-reaching organizational changes. Competitiveness demanded "structural adjustments" in the sense of New Public Management that were supposedly unavoidable. Hans Tuppy (ÖVP) – Minister of Science from 1987 to 1989 – stated in the 1987 University Report in the context of budget deficits and planned austerity measures:

---

116 *Amendment AHStG 1989*, §13 (a-c), RIS, https://www.ris.bka.gv.at/Dokumente/BgblPdf/19 89_2_0/1989_2_0.pdf (30 November 2021).

117 *Hochschulbericht* 1987, vol. 1, 403.

118 Dippelreiter, *50 Jahre*, 78–82; *Hochschulbericht 1981*, 138; *Hochschulbericht 1990*, vol. 1, 349–350.

119 Martin Winter, "Wettbewerb im Hochschulwesen," *Die Hochschule* 21 (2012) 2, 17–45, 17–18, University of Halle, https://www.hof.uni-halle.de/journal/texte/12_2/Winter.pdf (30 November 2021). Although he focused on German higher education institutions, similar tendencies can also be observed for Austria in the context of an increasingly international understanding of higher education.

"In an astonishingly rapid turnaround, probably accelerated by budget realities, politics has begun to demand efficient procedures determined by management methods even in the so-called protected areas of public administration […]. The prerequisites for a modern, mobile, international, and performance-oriented society also include an education system that promotes precisely these factors of mobility, internationality, and performance orientation."[120]

The gradual economization of the universities received a further boost after the end of the East-West conflict with the University Organization Acts of 1993 and 2002.[121] The idea that intensified international competition would promote "efficiency," "innovation," and "excellence" required increasing evaluation and standardization. The Bologna Process took further steps in this direction at the European level. The idea behind the harmonization of academic degrees and the introduction of ECTS was to make it easier for qualifications acquired abroad to be credited, to make achievements comparable, and thus to increase "mobility." As a result of international competition, educational migration gained increasing significance in three respects: at the individual level as a gain in experience and additional competence in the student's CV, at the institutional level in the form of figures in university rankings and a gain in academic expertise, and finally at the societal level through the expansion of national horizons and the pool of available labor. While for decades the idea prevailed that educational migrants would only stay in Austria temporarily as "guests" – even if the reality was different in many cases – a shift in perspective gradually set in here as well, as the state came to regard longer-term residency as an enrichment for the Austrian labor market.[122]

Despite increased internationalization, new dividing lines were established with Austria's accession to the European Union. While the free movement of persons has led to a strong increase in students from the EU, which is restricted only for certain subjects, third-country nationals continue to face more severe restrictions. In the context of the current anti-racist movement (Black Lives Matter), these existing inequalities have recently been questioned by the ÖH of the University of Vienna.[123] Inequalities have become particularly drastic in the context of Russia's war of aggression against Ukraine. While millions are fleeing the misery of the war and Ukrainian citizens in Europe are (still) meeting with a

---

120 Hans Tuppy, "Vorwort," in *Hochschulbericht 1987*, vol. 1, 11.
121 Jürgen Pirker, "Die 'Zeitenwende' an den österreichischen Universitäten. Umbrüche, Neuerungen und Folgewirkungen des UOG 1993," in Elmar Schübl/Harald Heppner (eds.), *Universitäten in Zeiten des Umbruchs. Fallstudien über das mittlere und östliche Europa im 20. Jahrhundert* (Vienna: LIT 2011), 107–120.
122 "Hochschulstudium und Internationalisierung von Lehre und Studium," Federal Ministry of Education, Science and Research, https://www.bmbwf.gv.at/Themen/HS-Uni/Studium/HSMob.html (1 December 2021).
123 ÖH Wien, "Rassismus an der Universität," ÖH, https://neu.oeh.univie.ac.at/politik/standpunkte/rassismus-der-universitaet (30 November 2021).

wave of solidarity, reports of discrimination against third-country nationals from Ukraine are increasing, including obstacles in crossing the border, racist insults, a situation of limbo in terms of residence law, and problems in finding accommodation and in taking up or continuing studies. It remains to be seen to what extent the buzzword "internationalization," which is often narrowly focused on economic benefits, can also be the starting point for a solidarity-based perspective of an inclusive academic community. This also includes awareness of the long transnational history of educational migration to Austria, its magnitude, and the traces it has left in Austrian society.

Wolfgang Mueller / Hannes Leidinger / Viktor Ishchenko

"When Israel Was in Egypt's Land." Jewish Emigration from the USSR, 1968–1991

At a gala dinner of about three hundred guests in Washington, D.C., on 27 October 1979, the conductor Leonard Bernstein raised his glass after a performance of Ludwig van Beethoven's only opera. As the son of Jewish immigrants explained, *Fidelio* is an expression of the "American dream," the dream that freedom, faithfulness and human rights will, in the end, prevail over oppression and tyranny. The opera tells the story of Leonore, who has disguised herself as a young man to become the prison guard Fidelio in an attempt to rescue her husband, a political prisoner. Together the couple succeeds in bringing the political suppression to the attention of the righteous minister Don Fernando, who appears at the climax of the opera and puts an end to all injustice. Turning to the Austrian chancellor who was in the United States for a three-day official visit, Bernstein said that despite Bruno Kreisky having often been "criticized by Jews in America and Israel," the social-democratic lawyer from an assimilated Viennese Jewish family was an "embodiment of this struggle for freedom and human rights." Bernstein's tribute culminated with the resounding statement: "Bruno Kreisky is Fidelio." Notwithstanding this being an obvious overstatement, the response to the conductor's emotional words was a standing ovation from the other guests, including the Secretary General of the United Nations Kurt Waldheim, former Secretary of State Henry Kissinger, several members of the US presidential cabinet, and two dozen members of the US Congress.[1]

A part of the conductor's generous praise for the Austrian head of government may have been earned by the fact that, from 1967 to 1990, more than half a million

---

1 Schober – Bundesministerium für Auswärtige Angelegenheiten (BMAA), Besuch Bundeskanzler Kreiskys in Washington, 5. Nov. 1979, Zl. 857-Res/79, Österreichisches Staatsarchiv, Archiv der Republik (ÖStA, AdR), BMAA, II-Pol 1979, GZ. 518.01.08/31-II.1/79. Sincere thanks go to Dr. Maximilian Graf for having shared this document with us. For a review of the Vienna Philharmonic's performance at the John F. Kennedy Center for the Performing Arts, see Paul Hume, A Radiant "Fidelio," in *The Washington Post,* 29 Oct. 1979. Available at: https://www.washingtonpost.com/archive/lifestyle/ 1979/10/29/a-radiant-fidelio/9fee251d-f018-4f62-b70c-2a9b445b181f/.

Jewish citizens of the Soviet Union emigrated abroad, most of them passing through Austria on their way.[2] Of these, 65 percent ultimately went to Israel.[3] It was one of the largest waves of Jewish migration in modern times. The previous wave of emigration starting with the pogroms around 1880, by World War I had led to the exodus of about two million of the five million Jewish citizens of the Russian Empire. The second wave, which increased significantly after 1967, contributed to the genesis of a post-Soviet global Jewish diaspora.

The wave would have certainly been much larger had the Soviet rules for leaving the country been less restrictive. Until 1989, emigration was possible only for some, and sometimes only after a long struggle. And yet, despite the possible dangerous consequences of applying for permission to leave the USSR, more than half a million requests were made between 1967 and 1990.

---

2 According to Petrus Buwalda, *They Did Not Dwell Alone: Jewish Emigration from the Soviet Union 1967–1990*, Washington, D.C.: The Woodrow Wilson Center Press 1997, 223 f, 527,234 Israeli visas were issued at the Netherlands embassy in Moscow in 1967–1990. This number, which is based on data from the Netherlands embassy in Moscow and Jewish organizations, for the years 1945–1980, roughly conforms with the Soviet figure of about 253,000 exit visas granted to Jewish citizens. B. Morozov, *Evreiskaya emigratsiya v svete novykh dokumentov*, Tel-Aviv: Ivrus, 1998, 17. The number of Jewish exits from the USSR for 1945–1985 is given as about 290,000 by P. Polyan, Emigratisya: Kto i kogda v XX veke pokidal Rossiyu, in O. Glezer/P. Polyan eds., *Rossiya i ee regiony v XX veke: territoriya – rasselenie – migratsii*, Moscow: OGI 2005, 493–519, 513. These numbers are significantly higher than earlier estimates, such as 240,000 for the years 1968–1989 by Zvi Gitelman, *A Century of Ambivalence: The Jews of Russia and the Soviet Union, 1881 to the Present*, 2nd ed., Bloomington: Indiana University Press 2001, 185. The same number and percentage, however, are given in documents of the Soviet Ministry of the Interior, but for the years 1970–1980 only. Ministerstvo Vnutrennykh Del – TsK KPSS, 10 Feb. 1981, in Morozov ed., *Evreiskaya emigratsiya*, 229. According to Soviet censuses, the Jewish community of the USSR shrank from 2.27 million in 1959 to 1.48 in 1989. M. Tol'ts, Evreiskaya demografiya: iz Sovetskogo proshlogo v postsovetskoe nastoyashchee, in M. Beizer ed., *Istoriya evreiskogo naroda v Rossii, t.3: Ot revolyutsii 1917 goda do raspada Sovetskogo Soyuza*, Moscow: Mosty kultury 2017, 433–452, 433. A recent calculation puts the number of émigrés at 360,000 for 1968–1989, which conforms to the data presented by Buwalda. G. Anderl/V.V. Ishchenko, Emigratsiya evreev iz Sovetskogo Soyuza i Avstriya, in A.O. Chubar'yan/S. Karner eds., *Rossiya – Avstriya: Vekhi sovmestnoi istorii*, Moscow: Aspekt Press 2018, 255–265, 257.

3 According to Buwalda, *They Did Not Dwell Alone*, 223 f, 563,215 Soviet Jewish citizens arrived in Vienna in 1971–1990. Other estimates for Jewish transmigration through Austria are about 250,000 in 1973–1988 by Heinz Fassmann/Rainer Münz, *Einwanderungsland Österreich? Historische Migrationsmuster, aktuelle Trends und politische Maßnahmen*, Vienna: Jugend & Volk 1995, 37; and 270,199 in 1968–1986 by Oliver Rathkolb, International Perceptions of Austrian Neutrality, in Günter Bischof/Anton Pelinka/Ruth Wodak eds., *Neutrality in Austria*, Contemporary Austrian Studies 9, New Brunswick: Transaction, 2001, 69–91, 82. These figures are roughly in line with Buwalda's estimates for these years. Cf. Vladimir Vertlib, *Osteuropäische Zuwanderung nach Österreich 1976–1991 unter besonderer Berücksichtigung der jüdischen Immigration aus der Sowjetunion*, Vienna: Verlag der Österreichischen Akademie der Wissenschaften 1995.

What were the reasons for this extraordinary level of migration? Why did the Soviet leadership sometimes liberalize the rules for emigration and sometimes tighten them again? And why did Austria become a transit hub for Soviet-Jewish migrants? This article will start with a brief look at the situation of the Jewish community in the USSR, and then analyze Soviet policies with regard to Jewish emigration. Here issues of why exit from the Soviet Union was either granted or refused will be dealt with on the basis of edited Soviet documents as well as accounts of Western eye witnesses. Due to the arcane character of Soviet politics, many eyewitnesses puzzled over the question of whether permission to leave was being granted mainly as a result of foreign-policy considerations, or rather due to domestic pressure. In the final section of the article, Austria's role as a transit point for hundreds of thousands of Soviet-Jewish emigrants will be examined. For this we draw on hitherto unpublished information from the Soviet consulate in Vienna.

The situation of the Soviet Jewry

The reasons after World War II that so many of the two million members of the Soviet Jewish community decided to make an attempt to leave their country were manifold and complex.[4] On 13 January 1948, the chairman of the Jewish Anti-fascist Committee, Solomon Mikhoels, died in Minsk in what looked like a car accident. Several months later, almost all of his colleagues were arrested, the Committee was dissolved, and Jewish cultural institutions were closed down. After the end of the USSR, archival documents became accessible proving that the car accident was staged by the Soviet secret police and that Mikhoels had been murdered on Stalin's orders. During the war, Mikhoels, the renowned head of the Moscow Yiddish Theater, had been quite successful in fulfilling the Committee's task of raising funds in the United States for the Soviet war effort.[5] After the war was won, however, both achievements – cultivating a specific national culture and networking abroad – became the target of Soviet suspicion. From 1946 onward,

---

4 According to Soviet censuses, about 2.27 million Jews lived in the USSR in 1959 (1970: 2.1 million), constituting about 1.9% (1970: 0.9%) of the Soviet population, with the largest communities in Ukraine (840,000; 1970: 500,000), Moscow (239,000/250,000), Leningrad (171,000/156,000), Belarus (150,000/148,000), Moldova (95,000/98,000), the Baltic republics (66,500/65,000) and Georgia (51,000/55,000). *Vsesoyuznaya perepis' naseleniya SSSR 1959 g.: Natsional'nyi sostav*, http://www.demoscope.ru/weekly/ssp/sng_nac_59.php; Andropov – TsK KPSS, 20 May 1972, with appendices, in Morozov ed., *Evreiskaya emigratsiya*, 136–148, 139.
5 Joshua Rubinstein/Vladimir P. Naumov eds., *Stalin's Secret Pogrom: The Postwar Inquisition of the Jewish Anti-Fascist Committee*, New Haven: Yale University Press 2001, 1f. Cf. Arno Lustiger, *Rotbuch: Stalin und die Juden: Die Tragische Geschichte des Jüdischen Anti-faschistischen Komitees und der sowjetischen Juden*, Berlin: Aufbau-Verlag 1998.

Soviet authorities and propaganda cracked down on anything that did not fit the new official line of Soviet nationalism and the special status of the Russian nation within it. Campaigns were launched against what was termed the "bourgeois nationalism" of the "smaller peoples" or the "national egocentrism" of Soviet Jews. In addition to this, the Committee's earlier contacts with the West fanned Stalin's suspicion that Committee members had become Western spies. When Israeli Ambassador Golda Meir was cheered in Moscow in September 1948 by enthusiastic members of the Jewish community, this seemed to confirm Stalin's mistrust of Jewish citizens.

The situation of the Soviet Jewry was exacerbated by developments in the Near East and the Soviet reaction to them. Until 1948, the USSR had supported the idea of creating a Jewish homeland abroad and thus it had not interfered in Jewish migration from Eastern Europe to Palestine or in the sale of arms from Eastern countries to Zionists. This certainly had to do with the Soviet aim of weakening British influence in the Near East and with Stalin's expectation that a new Jewish state would become socialist. Moreover, the USSR anticipated that Jewish migration to Palestine would come from Western countries, but not from the USSR. Similar expectations had been voiced in the war years in conversations with Soviet diplomats by the president of the World Zionist Organization Chaim Weizmann, who had expressed his opinion that Soviet Jewry would be assimilated within twenty to thirty years.[6]

After the creation of the state of Israel in May 1948 and its successful defense against Arab aggression in the first Arab–Israeli War, however, Soviet expectations and policy reversed. Israel was condemned as a bourgeois state. Soviet Jews were instructed not to even consider migrating to Israel and those who did express a wish to do so were arrested and accused of "bourgeois nationalism" and "Zionism." The change in Soviet relations with Israel went hand in hand with an increase in Stalinist pressure on the Soviet Jewry. From 1948 onward, thousands of the Jewish community's members and cultural figures were arrested, accused of made-up charges such as "slander of the USSR" or espionage, and sentenced in several trials to years of hard labor in Soviet prison camps.[7] Yiddish culture as a public phenomenon in the USSR was virtually destroyed. Moreover, in November 1948, a new, even broader campaign was launched in which Jews were stigmatized as "rootless cosmopolitans" and accused of being unreliable, treacherous and disloyal to the Soviet state. The Soviet press began to reveal the Jewish names of individuals who had adopted Russian ones. Anti-Semitic depictions of so-called

---

6 Morozov, *Evreiskaya emigratsiya*, 10 f. See also *Documents on Israeli-Soviet Relations 1941–1953*, vol. 1–2, London: Routledge 2000.

7 Gitelman, *A Century of Ambivalence*, 150–155. Cf. Benjamin Pinkus, *The Jews of the Soviet Union: The History of a National Minority*, Cambridge: University Press 1988.

"Zionists" appeared in the media. In July 1952, twenty-five prominent representatives of Jewish culture were put on trial and soon thereafter many were executed, among them the poet Peretz Markish and the pro-Stalinist Itsik Fefer. The anti-Semitic campaign spilled over into other Soviet-controlled communist countries, adding a twist to the trial of Rudolf Slansky in Prague from 20 to 23 November 1952, the last of a series of major Stalinist political trials in Eastern Europe. However, Stalinist terror was not yet exhausted. In January 1953, the arrest of a group of nine doctors, seven of them Jewish, was announced in Moscow. They were accused of having poisoned two members of the Soviet elite, the writer and politician Aleksandr Shcherbakov in 1945 and Stalin's heir apparent Andrei Zhdanov in 1948, on order of Western secret services. Soviet media did their best to present the accused as guilty and to incite general hatred against Jews, who were labelled "enemies of the people." The "anti-cosmopolitan campaign" led to what was described by contemporaries as a "pre-pogrom atmosphere" in Moscow and other places: Jewish persons were discriminated against, publicly attacked and harassed, children were beaten up, Jewish books were burned and objects were destroyed. Hundreds of Jews were fired from their jobs and arrested. Moreover, after an explosion in February 1953 at the Soviet diplomatic mission in Tel Aviv, the USSR severed diplomatic relations with Israel.[8]

Some historians have argued that Stalin planned to exterminate the Soviet Jewry in a second Holocaust.[9] While this cannot be proven, there can be no doubt that thousands, if not millions, of lives were saved by the dictator's sudden death in March 1953. One month later, investigations into the so-called "Doctors' Plot" were stopped, the arrested doctors were set free and those who had been convicted in anti-Jewish trials were rehabilitated, as were thousands of other victims of Stalin's terror. Diplomatic relations with Israel were already reestablished in July 1953. In a courageous step, Nikita Khrushchev, who emerged as the new leader in the subsequent power struggle, denounced Stalin's crimes and ended the mass terror. The physical threat to the survival of Soviet Jewry was over. Jewish cultural life recovered, albeit slowly and on a smaller scale. For ten years from 1958 onward, literature was again printed in Yiddish. From August 1961 the pro-regime journal *Sovetish heimland* was published, and in September of that year Yegenii Yevtushenko gave a public recitation of his poem *Babii Yar*, in which he called for an end to anti-Semitism in the Soviet Union. The first Hebrew-

---

8 Yosef Govrin, *Israeli-Soviet Relations, 1953–1967: From Confrontation to Disruption*, London: Routledge 1998.
9 Timothy Snyder, *Bloodlands. Europe Between Hitler And Stalin*, New York: Basic Books 2010, chapter 11.

Russian dictionary to be published in the USSR appeared in 1963.[10] However, soon thereafter two new campaigns were launched. The first was generally antireligious, but it used massive anti-Semitic and anti-Zionist imagery (some of it reminiscent of Stalinist propaganda) and led to the banning of religious traditions and the closing down of dozens of synagogues (as well as hundreds of mainly Orthodox churches). The second campaign was directed against economic corruption and led to more than four hundred trials. Among the accused were 1,676 Jews, of whom ten percent were shot. Various restrictions for Jews remained in place as well: careers in the party or the government, police, the army or as members of the diplomatic corps were off limits. Similarly, with an entire generation of communist administrators who had grown to adulthood under Stalin, prejudices persisted and anti-Semitism remained "deeply ingrained in Soviet society."[11] Moreover, the Suez War of 1956 and First Secretary Khrushchev taking the side of Israel's opponents put a further strain on Soviet–Israeli and Soviet–Jewish relations.

Khrushchev was demoted in 1964. Already in 1965, one of his two successors, Prime Minister Aleksei Kosygin, denounced anti-Semitism as alien to the Soviet world view. On 5 September of that year, *Pravda* rejected anti-Semitism as a "miserable fabrication of racism and national hatred."[12] However, the 1966 trial against the dissidents Yulii Daniel and Andrei Sinyavskii signaled the limits of this liberalization. Moreover, the Six-Day War of 1967, during which the USSR supported the Arab side, led to a new wave of anti-Zionist and anti-Jewish propaganda in the communist bloc. In reports by Soviet diplomats, the Jewish state was accused of following a "sharply hostile policy against our country" and depicted as a "marionette of Anglo-American imperialism."[13] In June 1967, the USSR again severed diplomatic relations, and no new exit visas to Israel were granted for the next year.

Domestic and foreign pressure for liberalizing emigration

In the meantime, two civil rights movements emerged in the USSR, one demanding the general safeguarding of human and civil rights, the other focusing on the human and cultural rights of Jews in the USSR, in particular, their right to

---

10 Gennadii Kostyrchenko, Politika sovetskogo rukovodstva v otnoshenii evreiskoi emigratsii posle XX s"ezda KPSS (1956–1991), in O. V. Budnitskii ed., *Evreiskaya emigratsiya iz Rossii 1881–2005*, Moscow: ROSSPEN 2008, 202–219, 202f.

11 Gitelman, *A Century of Ambivalence*, 160–173 (quote).

12 Quoted from Kostyrchenko, Politika sovetskogo rukovodstva v otnoshenii evreiskoi emigratsii, 205.

13 Morozov, *Evreiskaya emigratsiya*, 14.

emigrate.[14] From 1964 to 1968, Jewish cultural activities increased, including synagogue visits, Holocaust remembrance events such as at Babii Yar, and the private, illegal, printing of non-censored publications (*samizdat*). Nonetheless, the resolve of many Jewish citizens to leave the country was certainly strengthened by the Sinyavskii-Daniel trial, the new wave of anti-Israel propaganda, and the Leningrad trial of eleven men and women who had attempted to hijack a small plane to fly to Israel in June 1970. The trial took place in December of the same year: two persons were sentenced to death (commuted later to 15 years imprisonment); the others received prison sentences of 5 to 15 years.[15] As a result of the growing desire to emigrate, on 6 August 1969, 18 Georgian-Jewish families sent a letter to the UN Commission on Human Rights demanding the right to leave the USSR. While they were "the first to call publicly for free emigration,"[16] soon more letters were addressed to UN agencies and Jewish organizations by Soviet-Jewish citizens wishing to emigrate. In summer 1971, a hunger strike was organized at the Moscow Central Telegraph by Jewish activists demanding the right to leave the country.[17]

In the meantime, the general human rights movement in the USSR received significant impulses from the Prague Spring of 1968 and the Helsinki Conference on Security and Cooperation in Europe (CSCE) of 1973–1975. The issue of emigration was also on the movement's agenda. The Moscow Helsinki Group, which was initiated in May 1976 by the human rights activists Yurii Orlov and Andrei Sakharov, had been made aware of the issue by many Jewish members, including Mikhail Bernshtam, Yelena Bonner, Aleksandr Ginzburg, Vitalii Rubin, Anatolii Shcharanskii and Vladimir Slepak. Some had applied for emigration visas, but had been rejected.[18]

During this time, a number of organizations aimed at supporting the Jewish civil rights movement in the USSR were founded in Northern America and – to a lesser degree – in Western Europe. Until then, that had been a matter that the political Left in the West had been uninterested in. When in 1949 the American communist writer Howard Fast shared his uncertainty with party leaders about

---

14 Zvi Gitelman, Soviet Jews. Creating a Cause and a Movement, in Murray Friedman/Albert D. Chernin eds., *A Second Exodus: The American Movement to Free Soviet Jews*, Hanover: Brandeis University Press 1999, 84–93, 85–88.

15 Agentstvo pechati Novosti – TsK KPSS, 27 Jan. 1971, in Morozov ed., *Evreiskaya emigratsiya*, 86–87 notes 3 and 5. Kostyrchenko leaves it open whether the hijacking attempt was a provocation by the KGB. Kostyrchenko, Politika sovetskogo rukovodstva v otnoshenii evreiskoi emigratsii, 211.

16 Gitelman, Soviet Jews. Creating a Cause and a Movement, 85.

17 Kostyrchenko, Politika sovetskogo rukovodstva v otnoshenii evreiskoi emigratsii, 211.

18 Andropov – TsK KPSS, 15 Nov. 1976, in B.N. Bredikhin ed., *Lubyanka – Staraya ploshchad': Sekretnye dokumenty TsK KPSS i KGB o repressiyakh 1937–1990gg. v SSSR*, Moscow: Posev 2005, doc. 44.

whether to disclose postwar Soviet anti-Semitism to the Western public, he was told to keep quiet: "Russia is […] the only socialist country. That's more important."[19] This viewpoint changed, however, with the Slansky trial of 1952, which led to a demonstration in New York City organized by the Jewish Labor Committee. At the demonstration, an address by President-elect Dwight D. Eisenhower was read in which he condemned that the "communists, like the Russian tsars and the German Nazis, are using Jews as the scapegoats of their regime."[20] After the so-called "Doctor's Plot" was fabricated by the Stalinist regime in January 1953, about 3,500 people attended a protest rally in Manhattan.

In the early 1960s, various civic groups were established, such as the Cleveland Council on Soviet Anti-Semitism, the Philadelphia Committee to Protest Soviet Anti-Semitism, the US Union of Councils of Soviet Jewry, the National Conference for Soviet Jews, the Student Struggle for Soviet Jewry and the American Jewish Conference on Soviet Jewry (AJCSJ), some with the support of Israeli agencies and secret services, in particular the so-called "Lishka."[21] From 1964, the *Information Bulletin* of the US Department of State reported on the "mistreatment of Jews in the Soviet Union,"[22] and from 1969 onward, in the words of Henry Kissinger, the Nixon administration "had begun to make overtures to Moscow to ease Jewish emigration, emphasizing that such a policy would improve the atmosphere of US–Soviet relations."[23] In Israel, Prime Minister Golda Meir openly supported the cause of Soviet Jews willing to emigrate by reading their letters out loud at the Israeli Parliament and having copies distributed at the United Nations. In 1970, the World Presidium for Soviet Jewry was founded; its aim was to make the general public aware of the "prisoners of Zion." From 23 to 25 February 1971, the First World Conference on Soviet Jewry was held in Brussels. Around the same time, Western European communists, most notably the powerful French Communist Party, joined the criticism of Soviet migration policy.

As historian Albert Chernin has assessed it, "the impact of the World Conference [of 1971 on Soviet Jewry] was seen almost immediately after its adjournment. Indications emerged of some loosening of emigration policies. As many as 1,000 Soviet Jews emigrated in March. In April, it went up to 1,300. By the

---

19 Howard Fast's autobiography *Being Red* as quoted in Albert D. Chernin, Making Soviet Jews an Issue: A History, in Murray Friedman/Albert D. Chernin eds., *A Second Exodus: The American Movement to Free Soviet Jews,* Hanover: Brandeis University Press 1999, 15–69, 19. At the time, the USSR had imposed Stalinism on Mongolia and Eastern Europe and thus was, in fact, no longer the only communist country in the world.

20 Quoted from Chernin, Making Soviet Jews an Issue, 20.

21 Buwalda, *They Did Not Dwell Alone,* 37 f. Ha-Lishka le-Kishrei Mada (Bureau of Scientific Relations; Lekem) was an Israeli intelligence agency.

22 Chernin, Making Soviet Jews an Issue, 52.

23 Quoted from Buwalda, *They Did Not Dwell Alone,* 44.

end of 1971, the total for the year had reached more than 13,000 in contrast to about 4,200 in 1970."[24]

Soviet migration policy and its international context

Whether the Brussels conference was the main reason for Leonid Brezhnev liberalizing Jewish emigration is still unclear. The Israeli government had raised the issue of emigration with the Soviets for the first time in 1950.[25] In 1948/1949, of 26 applications to leave the USSR for Israel, only 6 were granted. A similar number of exit visas were approved in 1951/1952. The first significant rise in numbers occurred only the post-Stalin years. After Khrushchev was demoted in 1964, the annual number of Jews leaving the USSR increased sharply, to 1,444 in 1965 and 1,892 in 1966.[26] From 1945 to 1968, the total number of Soviet Jews who left their country for Israel had become 8,296,[27] when, in response to the Six-Day War in 1967, Soviet authorities interrupted Jewish migration for a year.

The reasons for Soviet restrictions against emigration were both ideological and political. First, Soviet ideology claimed that communism had solved all contradictions and particular interests within Soviet society,[28] and thus it was "believed that anyone wanting to leave their 'workers' and peasants' paradise' was committing treason. Emigration could be allowed, grudgingly and as a gift, not as a right, for only one reason – family reunion."[29] Second, Soviet authorities feared that granting Jewish migrants exit visas not only might stimulate the Soviet Jewry's wishes further, but might even trigger similar wishes among other national minorities such as Germans and Crimean Tatars, thus turning emigration into a factor of constant inner unrest. The third main reason for denying exit visas to Jewish citizens was also political and had to do with the Near East. Since Israel was perceived as an enemy and Jewish immigration "was one of the vital factors for Israel, the USSR strove at limiting it," as historian Boris Morozov has put it.[30]

What were then the reasons for this policy changing in the 1960s? Soviet reasons for allowing people to leave the country are usually explained in two ways: first, by the aim of getting rid of persons highly active in pursuing their

---

24 Chernin, Making Soviet Jews an Issue, 61.
25 Morozov, *Evreiskaya emigratsiya*, 11.
26 Gitelmann, *A Century of Ambivalence*, 174.
27 Spravka KGB, 9 May 1973; MVD – TsK KPSS, 10 Feb. 1981, in Morozov ed., *Evreiskaya emigratsiya*, 169; 230.
28 Morozov, *Evreiskaya emigratsiya*, 11f.
29 Buwalda, *They Did Not Dwell Alone*, 47.
30 Morozov, *Evreiskaya emigratsiya*, 15.

goals and thus seen as troublemakers by the Soviet authorities; second, by the aim of improving the Soviet image abroad and relaxing East–West relations. Both hypotheses are correct, as Soviet documents demonstrate. In their proposal "on the renewal of the exit of citizens of Jewish nationality for permanent residency in Israel," submitted in June 1968 and approved by the Politburo, KGB chief Yurii Andropov and Foreign Minister Andrei Gromyko argued that increasing the number of exit visas to 1,500 per year would (a) "enable us to rid ourselves of nationalistic people and religious fanatics who have a bad influence on their environment," and (b) "limit detractive claims in Western propaganda about discrimination against Jews in the USSR" and "receive positive approval in the eyes of the world public opinion."[31] There may have been other foreign-political aims as well. As historian Yaakov Roi has argued, permitting or restricting Jewish migration from the USSR to Israel provided the Soviet government with a lever (or more precisely, a carrot and a stick) in the Near East – not only with regard to Israel, but the Arab countries as well.[32] Indeed, Arab states were concerned by Jewish immigration into Israel. According to Soviet instructions, their leaders were to be calmed down with the argument that the number of exit visas was insignificant, and that most emigrants were women, the elderly, or people without military or technical educations. In a decree of 29 February 1972, entitled "On measures for fighting the hostile propaganda regarding migration to Israel," the CPSU Politburo instructed the Soviet authorities to inform the representatives of Arab states that the Soviet restrictions against Jewish migration were meant to prevent a rise in the Israeli military potential.[33]

Soviet exit permits, in the words of former Netherlands ambassador to Moscow Petrus Buwalda, thus "were granted not to please the emigrants but to impress Western public opinion and governments and to remove 'unruly elements.'"[34] He added that "it seems likely that one of the reasons why the Soviets allowed the first wave of emigration in the early 1970s was their desire to see a European security conference begin."[35] This may hold true as well. And yet, the policy of using emigration for political means was not undisputed in the USSR. In the Politburo, opinions were sometimes split between those who were more "liberal," like Prime Minister Aleksei Kosygin, former KGB head Aleksandr

31 Andropov/Gromyko – TsK KPSS, 10 Jun. 1968, in Morozov ed., *Evreiskaya emigratsiya*, 62.
32 Morozov, *Evreiskaya emigratsiya*, 17. Cf. Yaacov Roi, *The Struggle for Soviet Jewish Emigration, 1948–1967*, Cambridge: University Press 1991.
33 Vypiska iz protokola Sekretariata TsK KPSS, 29 Feb. 1972; TsK – Sovposol Algiers, Amman, Aden, Bagdad, Beirut, Damascus, Cairo, Kuwait, Rabat, Sanaa, Tripoli, Tunis, Khartoum; Vypiska iz protokola Sekretariata TsK KPSS, 22 Jun. 1973, TsK – Sovposol Amman, in Morozov ed., *Evreiskaya emigratsiya*, 131–133; 171–174.
34 Buwalda, *They Did Not Dwell Alone*, 74.
35 Ibid., 120.

Shelepin and his successor Yurii Andropov, who were ready to use emigration as a political instrument, and the more "rigid" fraction consisting of Secretary of Ideology Mikhail Suslov, Ukrainian party secretary Petro Shelest' and others who advised against it.[36] When détente with the United States started, the Soviet desire for preferential trade and US loans added to the Kremlin's readiness to "let the people go."[37]

From 1970 onwards, US–Soviet détente seems to have been a particularly strong incentive for liberalizing emigration. In 1971, more than 13,700 Jewish citizens left the USSR, in the following year over 29,800. In 1973 a total of 33,500 left.[38] Perhaps in response to this increase, on 3 August 1972 the Supreme Soviet adopted the decree "On the reimbursement of state expenses for education of Soviet citizens leaving for permanent residency abroad." This increased the costs of emigrating by a fee being charged based on the academic degree the emigrant had achieved. These fees ranged from 4,500 rubles to 19,400 rubles (that is, 2.5 to 11 times an annual average salary).[39] After the decree was enacted, education fees brought in revenues of about 4.5 million rubles for the rest of 1972[40] and 1.5 million for the first quarter of 1973. It is significant, however, that the number of visa applications of Jewish applicants, of whom 13 percent had higher education, did not drop.[41]

In response to the Soviet education fee, a draft amendment to the US Trade Reform Act was introduced to the US Senate on 4 October 1972 by Senator Henry Jackson and to the House on 10 October by Representative Charles Vanik. The draft amendment made it virtually impossible to grant most favored nation (MFN) status to any country that "denies its citizens the right or opportunity to emigrate" or "imposes more than a nominal tax on emigration." Its aim was to convince the Soviet government to drop the education fee.[42] Another draft amendment, brought forward by Senator Adlai Stevenson, limited US loans to the USSR over four years at 300 million US dollars, nonetheless still an impressive sum. The prospect of receiving MFN status and US export loans had been on the

---

36 Morozov, *Evreiskaya emigratsiya*, 19.

37 Sana Krasikov, Declassified KGB Study Illuminates Early Years of Soviet Jewish Emigration, in *Forward*, 12 Dec. 2007. Available at: https://forward.com/news/12254/declassified-kgb-st udy-illuminates-early-years-of-00966/.

38 Spravka KGB, 9 May 1973, in Morozov ed., *Evreiskaya emigratsiya*, 169.

39 Buwalda, *They Did Not Dwell Alone*, 90.

40 Kostyrchenko, Politika sovetskogo rukovodstva v otnoshenii evreiskoi emigratsii, 208.

41 Andropov – Kirilenko, 19 Mar. 1973, Spravka, in Morozov ed., *Evreiskaya emigratsiya*, 159f.

42 On the amendment, cf. William Korey, Jackson-Vanik: A "Policy of Principle", in Murray Friedman/Albert D. Chernin eds., *A Second Exodus: The American Movement to Free Soviet Jews,* Hanover: Brandeis University Press 1999, 97–114; and, in great detail, Pauline Peretz, *Let My People Go: The Transnational Politics of Soviet Jewish Emigration during the Cold War,* London: Routledge, 2017, 193–243.

agenda less than half a year earlier at Brezhnev's summit with US President Richard Nixon in Moscow held from 22 to 30 May 1972, in addition to signing the Strategic Arms Limitation Treaty and the Principles of International Conduct.

While Andrei Sakharov and other Soviet dissidents urged Congress to adopt the amendments, the Israeli ambassador and members of the US administration expressed reservations. In order to prevent the amendment's adoption and most likely with an eye on the upcoming summit with Nixon three months later, in March 1973 Brezhnev ordered the education fee to be waived, explaining this step in a Politburo session the following way:

> "In the [first] two months of 1973, 3,318 people emigrated, 393 of them with higher education, and paid 1,561,375 rubles. This is the general state of affairs. That is why the Zionists cry, Jackson leans on it, and Kissinger goes to [Soviet ambassador Anatolii] Dobrynin and says: 'We understand that is your domestic issue and we cannot meddle into it, we also have our laws.' Here is what he says: 'Help us in some way, Nixon cannot force the [Trade] Bill [through Congress], he is working among the senators.' What do we need this million [rubles] for? … Let 500 secondary people go, but no academicians. Let them say that we took nothing from them. Take some engineers with higher education, with no relation to state secrets, for instance from the food industry, but not the defense industry. Let the engineers also go for free. This is a temporary tactical maneuver."[43]

In a subsequent conversation with Kissinger in May 1973, Brezhnev confirmed an emigration quota of 36,000 to 40,000 per year. After the House of Representatives initiated the process of passing the amendments, Foreign Minister Andrei Gromyko agreed in April 1974 to 45,000 emigrants per year. This number was confirmed by Brezhnev to US President Gerald Ford at the Vladivostok summit from 23 to 24 November.[44] Nevertheless, the US Senate passed the Trade Reform Act with the Jackson-Vanik and Stevenson amendments on 13 December of the same year.

In the meantime, the Arab "Yom Kippur" War of 6–26 October 1973 against Israel had led to a sharp decrease in Jewish emigration from the USSR. The monthly number of exit visa applications fell significantly, from 1,690 in October 1973 to 917 in March 1974.[45] In the mid-1970s, after the Conference on Security and Cooperation in Europe (CSCE) had been held, freedom in the USSR diminished considerably, as did the number of travel permits. The Soviet regime lost no time in cracking down on human-rights activists and groups inspired by

---

43 Zasedanie Politburo TsK KPSS, 20 Mar. 1973, in Morozov ed., *Evreiskaya emigratsiya*, 165f. Cf. Il'ya Kuksin, Brezhnev i evreiskaya emigratsiya, in *Zametki po evreiskoi istorii* 15(87), Sep. 2007. Available at: https://berkovich-zametki.com/2007/Zametki/Nomer15/Kuksin1.htm.

44 Buwalda, *They Did Not Dwell Alone*, 100–102.

45 MVD, Shchelokov – TsK KPSS, 22 Apr. 1974, in Morozov ed., *Evreiskaya emigratsiya*, 193. Cf. Buwalda, *They Did Not Dwell Alone*, 127.

the Helsinki declaration.[46] In 1977, the leader of the Moscow Helsinki Group (and subsequently an Israeli minister), Anatolii Shcharanskii, was imprisoned and sentenced to thirteen years imprisonment. Later, the activist Ida Nudel was sentenced to four years. Further arrests involved Aleksandr Ginzburg and Yurii Orlov. In October 1977, Soviet physicist and dissident Andrei Sakharov appealed to all signatory states of the Helsinki agreement to protest the restrictions imposed by communist regimes on free emigration.

The situation improved briefly between 1977 and 1979, with the advent of the Carter administration raising Soviet hopes for US grain, technology and loans, as well as for a waiver of the Jackson-Vanik amendment.[47] The Belgrade CSCE from October 1977 till March 1978 may have also played a role in softening the Soviet approach.[48] In any case, in 1979 Soviet-Jewish emigration reached a new high, at over 51,000. But this was soon nullified by the Soviet invasion of Afghanistan and a new peak in the Cold War. In 1980, the number of travel permits was slashed by 60 percent and in 1981, by another 50 percent.[49]

The phases of temporary liberalization in Soviet emigration policy did not put an end to Soviet suspicion and instrumentalization of emigrants or attacks against them. Even in Khrushchev's "thaw" period, negative propaganda about emigration, smear campaigns about emigrants and Israel, and the smuggling of agents provocateurs into civil society organizations did not cease.[50] In response to the Six-Day War, attacks against an alleged "international Zionist conspiracy," such as in *Pravda* on 4 October 1967,[51] were particularly aggressive. Between 1971 and 1991, no less than 59 books and brochures demonizing Zionism were published in various languages in the USSR in a total of 2 million copies.[52] In 1983, an "Anti-Zionist Committee of the Soviet Public," with a permanent secretariat of thirteen staff members, was created by the CPSU Propaganda Department and

---

46 Svetlana Savranskaya, Human Rights Movement in the USSR after the Signing of the Helsinki Final Act, and the Reaction of the Soviet Authorities, in Leopoldo Nuti ed., *The Crisis of Détente in Europe: From Helsinki to Gorbachev, 1975–1985*, London: Routledge 2009, 26–40; idem, Unintended Consequences: Soviet Interests, Expectations, and Reactions to the Helsinki Final Act, in Oliver Bange/Gottfried Niedhart eds., *Helsinki 1975 and the Transformation of Europe*, New York: Berghan 2008, 175–190.

47 Buwalda, *They Did Not Dwell Alone*, 131.

48 Kerstin Armborst-Weihs, *Ablösung von der Sowjetunion: die Emigrationsbewegung der Juden und Deutschen vor 1987*, Münster: LIT 2001, 104; cf. Laurie Salitan, *An Analysis of Soviet Jewish Emigration, 1968–89*, New York: ProQuest 1992, 152f.

49 Gitelman, *A Century of Ambivalence*, 188.

50 Predlozheniya Komissii t. Mukhitdinova, 29 Jan. 1958, in Morozov ed., *Evreiskaya emigratsiya*, 27–31.

51 Chernin, Making Soviet Jews an Issue, 53.

52 Kostyrchenko, Politika sovetskogo rukovodstva v otnoshenii evreiskoi emigratsii, 216.

the KGB; on 21 April 1983 it was presented to the public.[53] With the help of Soviet officials, anti-Semitic right-wing organizations like "Pamyat'" (Memory) were created.[54] Moreover, the respective department of the KGB focused its activities on "disrupting emigrant, nationalist and in particular Zionist organizations."[55] Even earlier, the Helsinki Group had become a target of KGB measures,[56] including subversion through under-cover agents and smear campaigns about activists.

Covert Soviet endeavors against Jewish emigration were not limited to the territory of the USSR. At least three significant activities involved foreign countries. From 1973, the Soviet secret services extended their activities for "disrupting emigrant, nationalist and in particular Zionist organizations" to the World Jewish Congress (WJC) and other Jewish organizations.[57] It was planned to breach the headquarters of WJC, steal correspondence, and publish it in a distorted manner with the aim of compromising the organization and its members. The second vector of Soviet activities abroad against Jewish emigration involved the support of Arab terrorist groups, such as the Palestinian Liberation Organization (PLO). Such groups received political as well as material support, such as weapons and training facilities. The third vector involved planting Soviet agents in Western, Jewish and Israeli organizations by channeling them undercover to the West or Israel as Jewish emigrants.[58]

The visa process and the emigrant composition

Whatever the ups and downs in Soviet emigration policy and quotas, applying for exit visas remained cumbersome, complicated and potentially dangerous. "Soviet citizens regarded the Jews who were allowed to emigrate both with contempt and envy: contempt because those Jews were 'committing treason' by leaving; envy because they themselves were hardly ever allowed to travel to the West, let

---

53 Vypiska iz protokola zasedaniya Sekretariata TsK KPSS, 29 Mar. 1983, in Morozov ed., *Evreiskaya emigratsiya*, 238–240. Cf. William Korey, The Soviet Public Anti-Zionist Committee: An Analysis, in Robert O. Freedman ed., *Soviet Jewry in the 1980s. The Politics of Anti-Semitism and Emigration and the Dynamics of Resettlement*, Durham: Duke University Press 1989, 26–50, 46 f.

54 Kostyrchenko, Politika sovetskogo rukovodstva v otnoshenii evreiskoi emigratsii, 215.

55 Christopher Andrew/Oleg Gordiewsky eds., *Instructions from the Centre. Top Secret Files on KGB Foreign Operations, 1975–1985*, London: Hodder & Stoughton 1990, 7 and 19.

56 Andropov – TsK KPSS, 15 Nov. 1976, in Bredikhin ed., *Lubyanka – Staraya ploshchad'*, doc. 44.

57 Christopher Andrew/Wassili Mitrochin, *Das Schwarzbuch des KGB 2. Moskaus Geheimoperationen im Kalten Krieg*, Berlin: Propyläen 2006, 350 f.

58 Oleg Kalugin, *Spymaster: My 32 Years in Intelligence and Espionage against the West*, London: Smith Gryphon 1994, 193 f.

alone emigrate. No wonder that the Soviet bureaucracy, even when official policy authorized the granting of exit permits, did its utmost to make the departure of the Jews as difficult as possible."[59] Moreover, obtaining an invitation from Israel made it necessary to send letters abroad and to receive foreign mail, most of which was routinely intercepted by the KGB, thus potentially leading to police observation and in some cases criminal investigations or the loss of employment.

In addition to an invitation from a first-degree relative in Israel, further documents were needed: an application, a declaration of intent to leave the USSR, a CV and one's birth certificate, an attestation of character issued by the employer, the permission of one's parents, a certificate from the house committee of one's residence, etc. The passport fee was between 300 and 400 rubles, the fee for renouncing citizenship another 500 – in sum about six average monthly salaries (150 rubles). From mid-1972 to March 1973, also the above-mentioned education fee had to be paid. The visa process was regulated by a Decree of the Council of Ministers dated 1 January 1972.[60] A visa required an official declaration by the Soviet authorities about the applicant's eligibility for emigration. According to the Order of the Supreme Soviet of 17 December 1967, all permanent emigrants automatically lost their Soviet citizenship.

No one who had been in contact with state or military secrets was granted permission to emigrate.[61] However, an analysis of who was granted permission to leave and who was refused has not been fully undertaken. Published cases allow the preliminary conclusion that applicants with a high professional status were more likely to be refused, whereas applicants who were considered undesirable citizens due to their political opinions or their profession being in less demand were more likely to be granted an exit visa.[62] Thus it was only outwardly paradoxical when undesired persons were "rewarded" by being given permission to leave. Some of the most prominent "refuseniks" (*otkazchiki*), like Iosif Begun and the physicist Aleksandr Lerner, were refused for "regime" reasons, that is, they had worked at technical or military institutions.[63] In the 1970s, the percentage of refused applications rose: while in the period 1945–1974 approximately 99,500 exit visas were granted and 1,602 refused (1.6 percent), if one adds the next six years and looks at 1945–1980, 253,000 exit visas were granted and

---

59 Buwalda, *They Did Not Dwell Alone*, 47.
60 Kostyrchenko, Politika sovetskogo rukovodstva v otnoshenii evreiskoi emigratsii, 207–210.
61 Andropov/Shchelokov – TsK KPSS, 13 Dec. 1971, in Morozov ed., *Evreiskaya emigratsiya*, 126–127. Cf. Buwalda, *They Did Not Dwell Alone*, 51.
62 Andropov – TsK KPSS, 18 Mar. and 20 Apr. 1971, in Morozov ed., *Evreiskaya emigratsiya*, 95; 103.
63 Andropov – TsK KPSS, 20 May 1972, with appendices, in Morozov ed., *Evreiskaya emigratsiya*, 136–148, 137 f.

15,813 refused, making the number of refused applications rise to 6 percent.[64] In the first six months of 1982, as few as 34.2 percent of all applications were granted.[65]

After permission to leave the USSR for Israel was obtained from the Soviet Office for Visas and Registration (Otdel viz i registratsii, OVIR), the next steps for most applicants were acquiring an Israeli immigration permit at the Netherlands embassy, and then a transit visa at the Austrian embassy for travel via Austria. As the USSR severed diplomatic relations with Israel in June 1967 due to the Six-Day War, the Jewish state offered the Netherlands the task of representing Israel in the USSR, and this was accepted. Before the personnel of the Israeli embassy departed from Moscow, on 13 June it was agreed with the Dutch consul, *inter alia*, that Soviet applicants for visas to Israel would be advised to travel to Vienna, where there was "an Israeli committee" (the Jewish Agency for Israel) that would receive them. Moreover, loans would be granted to Jewish emigrants to cover the cost of a one-way trip by air to Vienna.[66]

Among those leaving in 1973, the largest groups were from Ukraine (10,800), Georgia (8,000), Moldova (3,900), Uzbekistan (3,000), Lithuania (2,000), Latvia (1,300) and Moscow (1,600).[67] About 35.8 percent were men, 38.8 percent women, and the rest, children under the age of 16; about 40 percent were pensioners and 14.8 percent had higher education.

In the decade of 1970 to 1980, 249,300 Jews left the USSR, representing 11.2 percent of the Jewish community. At the regional level, however, the exodus was even more significant: 55.8 percent of the Jewish community of Georgia left, 45.7 percent of the Lithuanian, 34.2 percent of the Latvian, 27.5 percent of the Moldovan and 15.3 of the Uzbek. While the share of emigrants in the Jewish community of Ukraine (11.4 percent) was approximately on a par with the union-wide level, in certain districts the share was significantly higher, such as the Carpathian region (55 percent), Czernowitz (48.1 percent) and Odessa (20.7 percent).[68] When viewing these developments in the long term, the shrinking of regional Jewish communities is even more apparent. According to Soviet censuses, the Jewish communities of the USSR and the Russian Federation both shrank by 35 percent, that of Belarus by 25 percent, Moldavia and Latvia both by

---

64 Morozov, *Evreiskaya emigratsiya*, 17. Buwalda, *They Did Not Dwell Alone*, 65, speaks of 11,000 refuseniks; Kostyrchenko estimates the number of refuseniks at 40,000. Kostyrchenko, Politika sovetskogo rukovodstva v otnoshenii evreiskoi emigratsii, 215.

65 Ministerstvo Vnutrennykh Del – TsK KPSS, 11 Aug. 1982, in B. Morozov ed., *Evreiskaya emigratsiya*, 235.

66 Buwalda, *They Did Not Dwell Alone,* 25 and 72.

67 Ministerstvo Vnutrennykh Del – TsK KPSS, Spravka, 28 Jun. 1973, in Morozov ed., *Evreiskaia emigratsiya*, 196–198.

68 Ministerstvo Vnutrennykh Del – TsK KPSS, 10 Feb. 1981, in Morozov ed., *Evreiskaya emigratsiya*, 229f.

33 percent, Ukraine by 42 percent, and Georgia and Lithuania both by 50 percent.[69]

Table 1: Jewish Emigration from the USSR 1945–1991

	Departure from USSR (Morozov)	Visa issued in Moscow (Buwalda)	Arrival in Vienna (Buwalda)	Arrival in Tel-Aviv (Buwalda)	Emigration from the SU (Tolts)
1945–1968	8,296				
1967		1,162		1,162	
1968		230		223	
1969	2,673	2,808		2,979	
1970	992	935		1,027	
1971	13,711	c. 14,000	13,022	12,966	
1972	29,821	31,413	31,681	31,432	
1973	33,500	34,778	34,733	33,283	
1974		20,146	20,944	17,065	
1975		13,209	13,221	8,293	291,000
1976		14,064	14,261	7,258	
1977		17,146	16,736	8,253	
1978		30,379	28,865	11,998	
1979		50,461	51,333	17,277	
1980		20,342	21,471	7,393	
1981		9,127	9,448	1,757	
1982		2,561	2,692	731	
1983		1,344	1,314	378	
1984		890	895	335	
1985		1,153	1,140	348	
1986		902	914	206	
1987		8,563	8,155	2,072	
1988		26,183	22,403	2,173	
1989		83,666	85,140	12,721	72,000
1990		until Aug. 141,572	184,847	184,681	205,000
1991					195,000
Total		527,034	563,215	364,965	763,000

Sources: Buwalda, *They Did Not Dwell Alone*, 221–224; Morozov, *Evreiskaia emigratsiya*; Tol'ts, *Evreiskaya demografiya*, 3.

---

69 Tol'ts, Evreiskaya demografiya, 434.

Passage through Austria

Most Jewish migrants from the USSR traveled via Austria, a passage that was recommended by the Dutch and Israeli authorities due to the country's location and the existence of Jewish refugee facilities in it. Soviet authorities did not object, most likely because they were interested in raising neutral Austria's international prestige in the West.[70] As in many other countries, anti-Semitism had had a long and sometimes violent history in Austria, and thus it seemed an unlikely choice as a refuge for Jewish emigrants.[71] In Austrian politics, anti-Semitic statements were made not only by right-wing politicians, but at times also by moderates and even by Bruno Kreisky himself. Indeed, in his first government the Jewish chancellor had given several of the ministries to former Nazi party members and relied on the support of the right-wing Freedom Party in Parliament. In his controversy with Simon Wiesenthal, Holocaust survivor and Nazi hunter, Kreisky went as far as saying, "if the Jews are a people, they are a bad one."[72]

However, for centuries Vienna had also had a tradition of attracting Jewish migration from Central Europe, whether as a transit hub or as a final destination. In the twentieth century, this had been the case particularly during World War I and in the aftermath of World War II. In the 1950s and 1960s, such Jewish migration persisted, albeit at lower levels. In 1956, 2,398 people used Austria as a transit step on their way from Central Europe to Israel, a number that quickly increased, reaching a climax in 1961 with 17,844 migrants. In 1969, the number was still high, namely 11,040. In the meantime, the number of Soviet migrants using the route increased steadily.[73] In 1960, only 106 Jewish migrants from the USSR had traveled via Austria; by the early 1970s the numbers rose steeply, to 13,082 in 1971 and 31,804 in 1973, almost all Soviet-Jewish migrants of those years.[74] From 1960 to 1973, more than 164,000 Jewish citizens emigrated from Eastern Europe by traveling to Austria, among them some 72,000 from the USSR. Most arrived by train and were taken care of by the Jewish Agency for Israel

---

70 Wolfgang Mueller, *A Good Example of Peaceful Coexistence? The USSR, Austria, and Neutrality 1955–1991,* Vienna: Verlag der Österreichischen Akademie der Wissenschaften 2011.
71 Evelyn Adunka, Antisemitismus in der Zweiten Republik. Ein Überblick anhand einiger ausgewählter Beispiele, in Heinz P. Wassermann, ed., *Antisemitismus in Österreich nach 1945. Ergebnisse, Positionen und Perspektiven der Forschung,* Innsbruck: Studienverlag 2002, 12–65.
72 Kreisky: "Die Juden – ein mieses Volk", in *Der Spiegel* 47, 16 Nov. 1975, https://www.spiegel.de/politik/kreisky-die-juden-ein-mieses-volk-a-4c081012-0002-0001-0000-000041376698.
73 *Die Ereignisse vom 28./29. September 1973. Ein Dokumentarbericht,* ed. Bundeskanzleramt, Wien 1973, 15.
74 Stiftung Bruno-Kreisky-Archiv (SBKA), Vienna, Länderboxen, UdSSR 7.

(JAFI) at Schönau castle, 30 km south of Vienna, which had been rented for this purpose since 1965.[75]

In the meantime, Austrian civil society and politics had become involved in the struggle for Jewish emigration from the USSR. In 1968, the Union of Jewish University Students had started an information campaign; in 1971, Austria's Jewish Community Organization, the "Israelitische Kultusgemeinde," founded the "Komitee für die Juden der Sowjetunion" (Committee for the Jews of the Soviet Union), and later supported the unofficial "Hilfskomitee für russische Juden" (Assistance Committee for Russian Jews). Austria's Kultusgemeinde also took part in the series of international conferences in Paris 1970 and Brussels 1971 dedicated to the situation of the Soviet Jewry. Also in 1971, a number of Austrian social democrats and trade unionists, including the president of the Austrian Federation of Trade Unions Anton Benya and former Vice Chancellor Bruno Pittermann, appealed to Soviet authorities to allow Jewish citizens to emigrate. The attempt was dismissed by Soviet diplomats in a conversation with the Austrian ambassador to Moscow as "Zionist propaganda."[76] Kreisky intervened in several letters to prime ministers Kosygin and Tikhonov on behalf of Shcharanskii,[77] Nudel,[78] and other individuals eager to emigrate. In 1982 alone, the number of hardship cases pending in Soviet–Austrian negotiations reached sixty. However, the success of the Austrian efforts was often described by diplomats as "disappointing,"[79] as seen in the Soviet handling of Kreisky's appeal to Soviet leader Yurii Andropov to let imprisoned dissident Yurii Orlov emigrate to Austria. On Andropov's order, the official letter was intentionally left unanswered by the Kremlin.[80] Due to his engagement for Soviet dissidents, a public lecture by Kreisky in Moscow was cancelled and the chancellor was criticized in the Soviet press.[81] Responses of this kind were not unusual. When Pierre Elliott Trudeau, the Canadian prime minister, wrote a letter to Andropov on behalf of Shcharanskii, Andropov ordered: "Reply to the Canadian: 'We don't need to

---

75 ÖStA, AdR, BMAA, II-pol, Israel 2/7, 1973, Zl. 49.105.
76 Quoted in Wodak – Kirchschläger, Streng Vertraulich, 2 Jun. 1971, ÖStA, AdR, BMAA, II-Pol, GZ. 105.880–6/71, Z.113.202. We are grateful to Dr. Maximilian Graf for having shared this information with us.
77 SBKA, Länderboxen, UdSSR 5.
78 Kreisky – Tikhonov, 19 Nov. 1982, in SBKA, Länderboxen, UdSSR 7.
79 Information Austrian MFA, 7 Oct. 1982, in SBKA, Länderboxen, UdSSR 7.
80 Kreisky – Andropov, 5 Jul. 1983, in Rossiiskii gosudarstvennyi arkhiv noveishei istorii (RGANI), Moscow, f. 89/op. 28/d. 26, 5. A note to Andropov originating from the central committee apparatus recommending leaving Kreisky's intervention without an answer bears the handwritten words "Soglasen [I agree]. Andropov." Information for Andropov, 29 Jul. 1983, ibid., f. 89/op. 37/d. 38, 2.
81 Rathkolb, International Perceptions of Austrian Neutrality, 81.

prove our humanity, Mr. Prime Minister. It is part of the very nature of our society.'"[82]

The fact that Austria had become a transit hub for Jewish migration was also noticed by Palestinian Arab terrorists, who on 28–29 September 1973, one year after the murderous attack on the Israeli Olympic team in Munich, kidnapped three Soviet-Jewish migrants and one Austrian customs officer at the railroad station Marchegg east of Vienna. Despite repeated warnings, after period of high alert, Austrian authorities had downgraded security measures for trains.[83] After consultations with Arab diplomats and brief negotiations, the Austrian government fulfilled the kidnappers' demand of closing down the Schönau refugee center. Originally, the terrorists had suggested trading the hostages for convicted Arab-Palestinians in Israeli prisons. Recent research has suggested that the Marchegg assault was planned as a diversionary tactic aimed at distracting the attention of Israeli secret services on the eve of the Arab attack in the Yom Kippur War, which started one week later, on 6 October.[84]

Despite these events, Austria did not change its practice of accepting Jewish refugees as transit migrants. Soon after Schönau was closed down, a new transit center was opened in the Babenberg Barracks of the Austrian Army in Wöllersdorf. This center remained operative until the JAFI rented a building of the Austrian Red Cross on Dreherstrasse in Kaiserebersdorf in the south of Vienna in 1974.

"Drop out" from emigration to Israel and re-migration

From 1974 onward, more and more Soviet emigrants did not continue from Vienna to Israel, but instead chose other final destinations, such as the United States, or decided to stay in Austria. The first time this share was more than 50 percent was in 1977. The highest point was reached in 1988, with over 90 percent not continuing on to Israel.[85] For the entire period of 1967–1990, the average so-called "drop-out" rate was 35 percent. In Vienna, persons were primarily taken

---

82 Quoted in Dmitri Volkogonov, *Autopsy for an Empire: The Seven Leaders Who Built the Soviet Regime,* New York: Free Press, 1998, 374.

83 Erklärung von Bundeskanzler Dr. Bruno Kreisky vor dem Nationalrat zu den Vorfällen am 28. und 29. September 1973, abgegeben am 23. Oktober 1973, in *Österreichische Zeitschrift für Außenpolitik* 5, 1973, 314–323, 315.

84 Thomas Riegler, *Im Fadenkreuz: Österreich und der Nahostterrorismus 1973 bis 1985,* Vienna: V&R unipress 2011, 119f.

85 Buwalda, *They Did Not Dwell Alone,* 223f. On this phenomenon, cf. in particular, Ruth Orli Moshkovitz, "'Ich bin nur froh, dass die Sowjetunion uns nicht zurückgenommen hat.' Vergeschlechtlichte Erfahrungen bucharisch-jüdischer (Re-) Migration," Univ. Vienna: MA thesis 2016.

care of by the JAFI, the Hebrew Immigrant Aid Society (HIAS), or the American Jewish Joint Distribution Committee. According to Soviet data, the length of their stay in Vienna varied between a minimum of one month for a visa to West Germany, and six to ten months for immigration documents to the United States, Canada or Australia.[86]

In the 1980s, more than 65 percent of Soviet émigrés changed their ultimate destination in Vienna while *en route* to Israel and chose to go to other countries instead, most to the United States, Canada, Australia and Western Europe. While Bukharan Jews from Georgia and Central Asia still preferred Israel, members of Ashkenazi communities favored other destinations.

Jewish migrants from the USSR were collectively accepted as refugees by the United States until 1978. Persons interested in continuing on to the United States were usually sent from Vienna to Rome, where an office of the US Immigration and Naturalization Service was located. Their transport to New York was largely financed by the US government.[87]

There were various reasons for deciding against continuing on to Israel or remaining in Austria: the Yom Kippur War, Israel's difficult economic situation, and more active policies of informing transit refugees that they were not obliged to go to Israel, but free to choose their final destination. For many Jewish emigrants, applying to go to Israel had seemed the only possible way to leave the USSR.

Similar reasons were given for another complex phenomenon, albeit on much smaller scale: re-migration from Israel to Vienna. Re-migrants named various reasons: Israel's hot climate, cultural differences, failure to integrate into Israeli society, unfulfilled expectations regarding welfare, too little support from the Israeli authorities, a life style too liberal for some or living conditions too Oriental for others, and again, the Yom Kippur War. In many traditional Jewish families, the eldest member made decisions for the family. Many such elders felt unable to cope with the challenge of integrating into Israel society and thus decided to leave, along with their families.[88]

From 1969 to 1971, re-migration was insignificant, according to KGB reports, with only 49 individuals returning to Vienna from Israel.[89] Re-migration increased in 1971; in 1973 the monthly average was 145 individuals, with a peak of 512 a month in 1975. After this, numbers fell significantly, becoming nearly zero

---

86 Konsul'skii otdel Posol'stva SSSR v Avstrii, Prava cheloveka i polozhenie v Avstrii byvshikh sovetskikh grazhdan evreiskoi natsional'nosti (spravka), 25 May 1982, in Arkhiv vneshnei politiki Rossiiskoi Federatsii (AVPRF), f. 66/op. 71/d. 32/p. 134, 29.

87 Buwalda, *They Did Not Dwell Alone*, 59 f.

88 Moshkovitz, "'Ich bin nur froh, dass die Sowjetunion uns nicht zurückgenommen hat.," 53–75.

89 Andropov – TsK KPSS, 31 Aug. 1973, in Morozov ed., *Evreiskaia emigratsiya*, 179.

in the 1980s. It is quite likely that this had to do with people deciding on other destinations while in Vienna. Once people realized they were free to choose where to go, migration to Israel decreased, as did re-migration.[90] The Soviet Consulate in Vienna estimated that in 1980/1981, about 50 families attempted to return to the USSR via Austria.[91] Most re-migrants had Transcaucasian or Central Asian origins and little education, ranging from three to eight years. In contrast, most of the migrants who went on to destinations other than Israel or stayed in Austria came from industrially developed regions or the western parts of Ukraine, and had intermediate or higher education.

It is possible that some re-migration was stimulated by agents provocateurs from the Soviet secret services assigned the task of creating trouble and discrediting Israel among Soviet Jewry. The practice of smuggling undercover agents into specific communities was a widespread phenomenon in the USSR. In the early period, accusations by re-migrants focused almost exclusively on Israel and followed the lines of Soviet anti-Zionist propaganda. Their statements at press conferences and in a 1977 appeal to UN Secretary-General Kurt Waldheim claimed that they had been victims of their "petty bourgeois mindset," they had allegedly been "deceived by Zionists," that Israel was a society of "capitalist slavery," that it forced citizenship on Soviet Jews, that they regretted having "betrayed the USSR," and that they sincerely hoped to find the "Messiah" by returning to the "motherland of socialism." Those who were allowed to re-enter the USSR were then used by Soviet propaganda. However, the USSR did not receive all of them back, and thus the Kremlin was soon also criticized for this. It is still unclear how many re-migrants returned to the USSR. Many received permanent residency in Austria, or left for North America.[92]

View into the late 1980s and conclusion

It was only after the new Soviet leader Mikhail Gorbachev introduced a new policy of détente and liberalization after 1985 that the situation of Jews in the USSR improved significantly. Jewish victims of the Holocaust could be commemorated, Jewish organizations received greater freedom, Jewish activists like Anatolii Shcharanskii and Ida Nudel were released. Finally, Jews were allowed to leave the country in larger numbers. The number of Jewish emigrants rose dramatically, from 914 in 1986 to over 8,000 in 1987, and then again more than

---

90 Moshkovitz, "Ich bin nur froh, dass die Sowjetunion uns nicht zurückgenommen hat", 41.
91 Konsul'skii otdel Posol'stva SSSR v Avstrii, Prava cheloveka i polozhenie v Avstrii byvshikh sovetskikh grazhdan evreiskoi natsional'nosti (spravka), 25 May 1982, in AVPRF, f. 66/op. 71/ d. 32/p. 134, 27.
92 Moshkovitz, "Ich bin nur froh, dass die Sowjetunion uns nicht zurückgenommen hat", 46–51.

twofold to almost 19,000 in 1988. In 1989, it jumped to more than 71,000 and in 1990 to over 213,000, with approximately 181,000 migrating to Israel.[93] After the Politburo adopted a new course vis-à-vis Israel in December 1989,[94] on 18 October 1991 the Soviet Union resumed diplomatic relations with the country, ending a long period of tense or even hostile rejection.

Almost exactly a year earlier, on 14 October 1990, Leonard Bernstein, the great Jewish American conductor whose own emigrant father had come from Rivne, in today's Ukraine, had passed away in New York City, after an exceptionally rich life overflowing with emotion, compassion and artistic mastery. Had he lived to see these events, he might have raised his glass to Mikhail Gorbachev, praising the Soviet leader as *Fidelio's* Don Fernando.

* * *

After World War II, the Soviet approach to the fate of Soviet Jews swung between phases of repression and of relative liberalization. The Soviet decision to let some Jews leave the country was connected to aims of getting rid of troublemakers, fostering détente with the West, and harvesting Western loans. This commitment to migration however proved unstable, easily falling victim to international developments or other considerations.

That Austria was chosen as a transit point was most likely a result of the country's location as the easternmost outpost of the Western world, its infrastructure for supporting refugees, its travel connections and, for the most part, intact political relations with the Soviet Union, Israel and the United States, despite periodic tensions with the USSR and Israel. While most of the work of supporting the transit refugees was undertaken by Israeli and US organizations, there were also a few Austrian NGOs involved.

With increasing freedom to choose their final destination and as a consequence of other factors, more and more migrants chose to go to places other than Israel. With this development, the phenomenon of re-migration ceased to exist.

What did not end with perestroika nor with the dissolution of the USSR, however, was the flow of Jewish migration from the post-Soviet space to Israel and the West.[95]

---

93 Gitelman, *A Century of Ambivalence*, 194.

94 Vypiska iz protokola zasedaniya Politburo TsK KPSS, 29 Dec. 1989, in Morozov, *Evreiskaya emigratsiya*, 243–247. Cf. Aryeh Levin, *Envoy to Moscow: Memoirs of an Israeli Ambassador, 1988–92*, London: Routledge 1996.

95 Mark Tolts, Post-Soviet Aliyah and Jewish Demographic Transformation, Paper presented at the 15th World Congress of Jewish Studies, Jerusalem, 2–6 Aug. 2009. Available at: https://archive.jpr.org.uk/download?id=3233.

Maximilian Graf

Humanitarianism with Limits: The Reception of Refugees from the Global South in Austria in the 1970s[*]

Introduction

Since the so-called "refugee crisis" of 2015, Austrian studies about the history of migration have experienced a boom and an unprecedented number of edited volumes and themed journal issues on this topic have been published.[1] Most focus on contemporary history. Regarding Austria's role as a refuge during the Cold War, recent studies have aimed to critically reassess the country's record and bring the research up to the early 1990s. Building on the findings of the first critical studies published in the mid-1990s,[2] scholars have analyzed the contested reception of refugees from Poland in 1981/82[3] and Romania in 1989/90,[4] chal-

* This article is a result of the project "Unlikely refuge? Refugees and citizens in East-Central Europe in the 20th Century." The "Unlikely refuge?" project has received funding from the European Research Council (ERC) under the European Union's Horizon 2020 research and innovation program (grant agreement No 819461).

1 Günter Bischof and Dirk Rupnow (eds.), *Migration in Austria* (New Orleans: UNO Press, 2017) (Contemporary Austrian Studies 26); Börries Kuzmany and Rita Garstenauer (eds.), *Aufnahmeland Österreich. Über den Umgang mit Massenflucht seit dem 18. Jahrhundert* (Vienna: Mandelbaum, 2017); Stefan Karner and Barbara Stelzl-Marx (eds.), *Migration. Flucht – Vertreibung – Integration*, (Graz: Leykam, 2019); Senol Grasl-Akkilic et al. (eds.), *Aspekte der österreichischen Migrationsgeschichte* (Vienna: Edition Atelier, 2019). Also see the themed issue of *Österreichische Zeitschrift für Geschichtswissenschaften* 31 (2020) 1. For a full assessment of the state-of-the-art on Austria as a refuge in the Cold War, see Maximilian Graf, "Austria as a Cold War Refuge – Reassessing the Historiography," *Zeitschrift für Ostmitteleuropaforschung* (forthcoming 2022).

2 Brigitta Zierer, "Willkommen *Ungarnflüchtlinge* 1956?," in *Asylland wider Willen: Flüchtlinge in Österreich im europäischen Kontext seit 1914*, edited by Gernot Heiss and Oliver Rathkolb (Vienna: Dachs, 1995), 157–171; Patrik-Paul Volf, "Der politische Flüchtling als Symbol der Zweiten Republik: Zur Asyl- und Flüchtlingspolitik seit 1945," *zeitgeschichte* 22 (1995) 11/12: 415–436.

3 Sarah Knoll, "Flucht oder Migration? Polnische Flüchtlinge in Österreich 1981/82," in *Österreich – Polen. Stationen gemeinsamer Geschichte im 20. Jahrhundert*, edited by Peter Ruggenthaler and Wanda Jarząbek (Graz: Leykam, 2021), 223–238; Maximilian Graf, "Fluchtbewegungen nach Österreich im Zuge der 'polnischen Krise' 1980–1982," in *Migration. Flucht - Vertreibung - Integration*, edited by Stefan Karner and Barbara Stelzl-Marx (Graz: Leykam, 2019), 123–136.

lenging the notion of a consistently welcoming Austrian attitude toward refugees from communist countries. The initial humanitarian efforts in 1956, after the Soviet crackdown on the Hungarian uprising, and on later occasions were without a doubt remarkable. Indeed, throughout the Cold War, hundreds of thousands of Eastern Europeans were granted asylum in Austria or transited the country. However, an analysis that looks beyond the first weeks of the most well-known refugee and "welcome culture" moments of Austrian history reveals that public and political attitudes toward refugees tended to take a negative turn. This pattern has become more visible since the early 1980s and can be seen to this day.[5]

Despite remarkable progress in historical research regarding Austria as a refuge, the global dimension is still understudied. In the 1970s, Austria received Chilean, Cuban, Kurdish, Ugandan Asian, and Indochinese refugees.[6] This article offers the first assessment of the reception of non-European refugees based on archival research.[7] After a brief discussion of Austria as a refuge in the Cold War between myth and reality, it presents case studies on the reception of Chilean and Indochinese refugees. On the one hand, the focus is on the perspective of authorities driven by budgetary limit as well as various other concerns and the

---

4 Sarah Knoll, "Österreichs 'humanitäre Tradition'? Asyl- und Flüchtlingspolitik zwischen regionalen Reaktionen und globalen Veränderungen," in *Geschichte und Region/Storia e Regione* 30 (2021) 2: 41–62.

5 For a critical reassessment, see Maximilian Graf and Sarah Knoll, "In Transit or Asylum Seekers? Austria and the Cold War Refugees from the Communist Bloc," in *Migration in Austria*, edited by Günter Bischof and Dirk Rupnow (New Orleans: UNO Press, 2017), 91–111.

6 Homayoun Alizadeh, "Österreichische Flüchtlingspolitik der 70er Jahre," in *Asylland wider Willen*, 188–194. which is little more than a summary of Eduard Stanek, *Verfolgt Verjagt Vertrieben. Flüchtlinge in Österreich von 1945–1984* (Vienna: Europaverlag, 1985), 95–139, 155–167. When published the book was considered "emphatic." Today's reader would likely beg to differ; however, it still is an informative memoir and revealing of the attitude of the Austrian authorities. On the Kurdish diaspora in Austria, see Thomas Schmidinger, "Von den kurdischen Bergen in die Alpen – Vom Tigris an die Donau. Kurdinnen und Kurden als Teil der Migrationsgeschichte und Diversität Österreichs," in *Aspekte der österreichischen Migrationsgeschichte*, 270–283.

7 The availability of archival sources on refugee matters in the 1970s is still unsatisfying. Beyond the early 1970s no documents produced by the ministry of the interior have been declassified or transferred to the Austrian State Archives. Furthermore, in the late 1970s, the foreign ministry reorganized its structure and transferred all its documents on refugee affairs since 1960 to its Section IV whose documentation also has not yet been transferred to the Austrian State Archives. Fortunately, the documents produced by Section II (which are fully available in the archives) contain some copies of documents from and correspondence with Section IV as well as the Ministry of the Interior. This collection and archival documents from the Kreisky Archive provide the basis for this study. Kreisky's papers also contain materials produced by the Sections II and IV of the foreign ministry and the ministry of the interior. Furthermore, Kreisky's correspondence with citizens and NGOs and the material produced by them, provide insights into the growing role of non-state actors in refugee affairs. Kreisky's responses (drafted by his staff or the responsible ministries) show how politicians tried to explain their politics in refugee matters to informed people.

international workings of refugee resettlement. On the other hand, this study evaluates the impact of global human rights activism,[8] especially evident in the role played by activists, churches, and NGOs with transnational links, thinking globally and acting locally.

The admission of Chilean refugees following the coup against Salvador Allende in 1973 reversed the predominant pattern of welcoming refugees from communist countries. This group of refugees represented a varied sample of the Chilean left. Their reception caused diverging reactions among activists, refugees, and officials. Some publications offer insight into Austrian attitudes. For example, Sigrun and Herbert Berger, former activists from the Austrian "Chile Solidarity Front," have published on the reception and the trajectories of Chilean refugees.[9] Additionally, studied through the lens of state produced sources, we gain insights into Austrian dealings with non-communist dictatorships and can identify parallels to the approach taken in relations with Eastern Europe.

The case of the Indochinese refugees was closer to the Austrian experience of welcoming refugees who had escaped communist rule. It is of special interest, not least because solidarity with the "boat people" (who had become the subject of global media coverage and triggered refugee aid from civil society) overlapped with the next major influx of refugees from Eastern Europe, showing a significant shift in public and political reaction in Austria as well as in international resettlement practices. The conclusion places the findings from the two case studies squarely within the dominant focus on East-West migration, which shaped Austria's Cold War refugee policies the most.

Neutral Austria as a Refuge in the Cold War: Myth and Reality

In 1955, Austria regained its sovereignty with the signing of the State Treaty and adopted a neutrality law.[10] It did not take long before Austria's new status was put to a test when the Soviet Union violently suppressed the Hungarian uprising in autumn 1956, causing 180,000 people to flee to Austria. All of them were granted

---

8 Akira Iriye et al. (eds.), *The Human Rights Revolution. An International History* (New York: Oxford University Press, 2012).

9 Sigrun and Herbert Berger (eds.), *Zerstörte Hoffung, gerettetes Leben. Chilenische Flüchtlige und Österreich* (Vienna: Mandelbaum, 2002); Herbert Berger, *Solidarität mit Chile. Die österreichische Chile-Solidaritätsfront 1973–1990* (Vienna: Edition Volkshochschule, 2003). Sociological studies were devoted to the second generation of Chileans in Austria, see Katharina Kaudelka, *Übersetzungen. Lebenskonstruktionen in der zweiten Generation chilenischer Flüchtlinge* (Innsbruck: StudienVerlag, 2007).

10 Gerald Stourzh and Wolfgang Mueller, *A Cold War over Austria. The Struggle for the State Treaty, Neutrality, and the End of East-West Occupation, 1945–1955* (Lanham, MD: Lexington Books, 2018).

political asylum, however only a small percentage of them stayed in Austria permanently. International anti-communist solidarity secured a fast onward journey for almost all of the refugees.[11] Serving as state secretary for foreign affairs, Bruno Kreisky was conscious of the international reputation Austria had earned in the West and advocated for a new role for the country in the world. Akin to Switzerland as the home of the Red Cross, he opined that Austria could prove itself to the world as an asylum-granting country.[12] All escapees from communist rule were considered political refugees, regardless of their actual motivations. According to Emmanuel Comte, their swift resettlement in the West aimed at stabilizing West Germany and other countries bordering the Eastern bloc, not least Austria.[13]

Against this backdrop, the Alpine Republic cultivated its image as a country of first asylum for refugees from communism. Until 1968, the annual influx amounted to only approximately 4,000 people, a large majority of whom were granted political asylum.[14] After the crushing of the "Prague Spring," at least 162,000 people reached Austria. A total of 12,000 Czechs and Slovaks applied for political asylum in Austria, and it is estimated that only 2,000 to 3,000 remained permanently.[15] Throughout the 1970s, asylum for dissidents was portrayed as a continuation of the country's humanitarian tradition.[16] Nevertheless, Austria regarded itself primarily as a transit country, and it served as such by facilitating Jewish emigration from Eastern Europe.[17] Whenever Austria faced a "refugee crisis," it called for international support, and until the late 1970s, the West responded accordingly.[18] However, it must be noted that from an Austrian perspective, aid and resettlement never happened quickly enough. Additionally, the country was left with the impression that recipient countries were picking the best people, whereas Austria was left with those no one else wanted. Knowing the importance of quick resettlement in times of massive influx of refugees, one would expect a thorough understanding for other first asylum countries and

---

11 Andreas Gémes, *Austria and the 1956 Hungarian Revolution: Between Solidarity and Neutrality* (Pisa: Univ. Press, 2008).

12 Bruno Kreisky, *Im Strom der Politik. Erfahrungen eines Europäers* (Berlin: Goldmann, 1988), 231.

13 Emmanuel Comte, "Waging the Cold War: The Origins and Launch of Western Cooperation to Absorb Migrants from Eastern Europe 1948–57," *Cold War History* 20 (2020) 4: 461–481.

14 Stanek, *Verfolgt Verjagt Vertrieben*, 82–86.

15 Silke Stern, "Die tschechoslowakische Emigration: Österreich als Erstaufnahme- und Asylland," in *Prager Frühling: Das internationale Krisenjahr 1968*, edited by Stefan Karner et al. (Vienna: Böhlau, 2008), 1025–1043.

16 Benjamin Gilde, *Österreich im KSZE-Prozess 1969–1983: Neutraler Vermittler in humanitärer Mission* (Munich: Oldenbourg, 2013), 289–304.

17 See the article by Wolfgang Mueller, Hannes Leidinger, and Viktor Ishchenko in this issue.

18 Sarah Knoll, "Calling for Support: International aid for refugees in Austria during the Cold War," in *zeitgeschichte* 48 (2021) 3: 387–407.

swift assistance during crises. However, this was not the case. Until the 1970s, whenever Austria was approached by the international community, it never admitted refugees from the Global South. The excuse usually was that the country was already overburdened by hosting refugees from Eastern Europe. For the same reason, Vienna's financial contributions to international refugee aid never reached the levels of similar states.[19]

Despite an ever-present focus on the cost of refugee aid and reception as well as limited political will for increasing financial means, the 1970s also brought change to Austria. Of course, parts of the Austrian left had engaged in solidarity with Algeria during decolonization and, naturally, humanitarian disasters like Biafra surfaced in the media, but, in general, the Global South had not taken center stage in the Austrian public sphere of the 1960s. No doubt, the Vietnam War as a global factor also influenced developments in Austria, and the world prepared for more disasters that would spur a global outcry and required an international response. In 1967, the Geneva Refugee Convention was stripped of its geographical limitations, and the 1970s saw a rise in global human rights activism. Austrian Chancellor Bruno Kreisky (who took office in 1970) was personally interested in the North-South-dimension of global politics and received a lot of international attention for his policies in the Middle East. This resulted in a diversification and internationalization of Austria's foreign policy.[20] Although the country's human rights and refugee policies were primarily conditioned by the East-West dimension of the Cold War, a global dimension was added in the 1970s that included the reception of non-European refugees.[21]

In 1972, Austria received 1,533 Asian refugees who had been expelled from Uganda by the dictator Idi Amin. The fate of these postcolonial and mostly stateless refugees became an international humanitarian concern. Also, in the case of the first significant cohort of non-European refugees, Austria regarded itself primarily as a port of transit. In the end, hardly any of the Ugandan Asians wanted to stay permanently and aimed for resettlement to English speaking countries instead. Most succeeded in the long term. Support for these refugees was facilitated by substantial assistance from the United Nations High Commissioner for Refugees (UNHCR), however, the costs covered by Austria were

---

19 As internal discussions and correspondence of the foreign ministry reveal, the Austrian government must have been fully aware of this fact. For example, see Memo to the Ministry of Finance "Freiwillige österr. Beitragsleistungen für die VN; Vergleich mit anderen Staaten," Österreichisches Staatsarchiv (ÖStA), Archiv der Republik (AdR), Bundesministerium für Auswärtige Angelegenheiten (BMAA), II-Pol, GZ. 423.14/6-II.5/78.

20 Elisabeth Röhrlich, *Kreiskys Außenpolitik. Zwischen österreichischer Identität und internationalem Programm* (Göttingen: V&R *unipress*, 2009), 301–342.

21 Maximilian Graf, "Beyond Victims of Communism? Austria and the human rights question in the 1970s" in *The Human Rights Breakthrough of the 1970s. The European Community and International Relations*, edited by Sara Lorenzini et al. (London: Bloomsbury, 2022), 178–195.

meticulously noted by officials who had the impression of ungrateful refugees. The initial aim of recruiting up to 200 carefully picked stateless refugees as part of the workforce led to the construction of twenty housing units on the premises of the former artillery barracks in Kaiserebersdorf. Their completion in 1975 came too late for those Ugandan Asians who settled in Austria but were desperately needed when Chilean and Indochinese refugees arrived.[22]

When Austria began to participate in global refugee management, the refugee situation in the country was relaxed. Without major crises, the annual influx of Eastern Europeans never exceeded several thousand refugees and was considered manageable. The economy was still booming, and the country actively recruited foreign labor to satisfy demand. Foreign labor in Austria reached a first peak in 1973 with 230,000 foreign workers representing almost 9 percent of the total workforce. The first "oil shock" resulted in a recruitment stop and a freeze of the number of foreign workers at the 1973 level, gradually reducing the acceptance of foreign workers in Austria not least by the traditionally deprecatory trade unions. When xenophobic tendencies surfaced in Austrian society, the government countered by referring to the country's multinational legacy stemming from the Habsburg Empire. The economic situation in Europe was aggravated after the second "oil shock" of 1979. In the case of Austria (with a strong but largely unreformed nationalized industrial sector), this brought a definitive end to full-employment and, as a consequence, reduced the acceptance of foreign competitors on the job market. This domestic development was accompanied by a substantial increase in asylum seekers from Eastern Europe in the late 1970s. From summer 1980 onward, the independent trade union Solidarity posed a growing challenge to the Polish regime. In the end, the communist leadership decided to impose martial law in December 1981. Throughout the year 1981, the number of Polish asylum seekers in Austria grew exponentially. However, from the start, considerable segments of Austrian society regarded the Poles as unwelcome labor migrants. Austria's tabloid press pressured the government to take action. The government stopped the influx by suspending visa-free travel, which had been in effect since 1972 for Poland. The public at large only became more accepting of refugees after martial law was imposed. A national aid committee was formed and collected donations. However, the solidarity with those who stayed in Austria was short-lived. As in 1956 and 1968, Austria wanted to serve as a transit country only and demanded international assistance. This time, however, the international community was less responsive, and many refugees

---

22 Stanek, *Verfolgt Verjagt Vertrieben*, 98–111; Sara Cosemans, "The politics of dispersal: Turning Ugandan colonial subjects into postcolonial refugees (1967–1976)," *Migration Studies* 6 (2018) 1: 99–119. On Austrian labor recruitment interests, see Staribacher diaries, 25.9. and 7.11. 1972. For the online edition, see Tagebücher Josef Staribacher. Digitale Ausgabe. Ed. by the Kreisky-Archiv and ACDH (https://staribacher.acdh.oeaw.ac.at/).

remained in Austria indefinitely.[23] Unsurprisingly, this affected the Austrian attitude toward refugee admission, especially from the Global South, and serves as an important context for the following case studies.

The Reception of Chilean Refugees: From Asylum in the Embassy to Tank Exports

On 11 September 1973, a coup by the Chilean military violently ended civilian rule by President Salvador Allende and his Unidad Popular government. Although Austrian public opinion was divided in its interpretation of events in Chile, the voices opposing the junta led by general Augusto Pinochet were strong. Soon, reports about human rights violations in Chile shaped the news. Activists called on the Austrian chancellor to take a stance and to invite Chilean refugees to Austria.[24] The government condemned the military takeover and noted that any impression of recognizing the junta was to be avoided by all possible means. At the same time, contacts with the Chilean authorities were maintained to protect Austrian interests[25] and to conduct humanitarian interventions.

On 13 September 1973, Amnesty International's (AI) International Council Meeting convened in Vienna. Chancellor Kreisky gave a welcome address in which he wholeheartedly identified with the aims and intentions of the organization. His own biography made him a perfect advocate for the cause of AI. In the interwar period, Kreisky had been persecuted by the Austrian dictatorship. After Austria's annexation by Nazi Germany in 1938, he found refuge in Sweden. Since the 1950s, Kreisky had decisively shaped Austrian foreign policy. During détente's heyday in Cold War Europe, his approach to humanitarian engagement was dialogue and discretion rather than public polemics. Kreisky exemplified this in his address at the AI meeting by mentioning the dissident Andrey Sakharov and the need to unambiguously explain to Soviet leaders that human rights violations constituted obstacles to increasing East-West exchanges and cooperation in the fields of science and culture. Toward the end of his speech, the chancellor remarked "that one cannot remain silent on events in Chile and the death of Allende, for many reasons and not least because otherwise one would lose the moral right to stand up for Sakharov and his fellow combatants."[26] It was

---

23 Graf, "Fluchtbewegungen nach Österreich im Zuge der 'polnischen Krise' 1980–1982."
24 See documentation in Kreisky-Archiv, Box Chile 1, folder 1973.
25 Memo "Chilenischer Staatsstreich; Möglichkeit der Notifizierung der Regierungsübernahme durch die Junta," Vienna, 14.9.1973, ÖStA, AdR, BMAA, II-Pol, Chile 3, GZl. 30.482/7/73, GZ. 44.993–7(Pol)/73.
26 "Tagung des Internationalen Rates von Amnesty International, 13 September 1973," in *Kreisky Reden*, vol. II (Vienna: Verlag der Österreichischen Staatsdruckerei, 1981), 330–332.

a mere coincidence that the AI meeting took place shortly after the coup against Allende. Nevertheless, Kreisky's speech and the time it was given are revealing about the Austrian dealing with the question of human rights on an international scale and the changes it underwent. It shows the anti-communist Cold War origins and the degree of universality human rights had reached at the time.

Since the Austrian ambassador in Santiago de Chile, Adolf Hobel, who held a very negative view of Allende's politics, was reluctant to grant asylum on his premises, he was immediately replaced. The chargé d'affaires, Paul Leifer, opened the Austrian Embassy for those who feared persecution, and the government decided to welcome 200 refugees from Chile. The life-long anti-communist Kreisky personally appealed to Pinochet to prevent the expected execution of the incarcerated leader of the Chilean Communists Luis Corvalán. Many more interventions in favor of imprisoned (mostly socialist) politicians by Kreisky and other Austrian politicians followed. Austria offered asylum in the case of their release and expatriation by the junta.[27] As long as the refugees in the embassy were not permitted to leave for Austria, the new Chilean ambassador in Vienna had to wait for his agrément. Exerting pressure was one layer to add authority to humanitarian efforts,[28] the continuation of certain contact with the junta the other.[29]

Despite many appeals from the public, Austria did not sever diplomatic relations with Chile because this would have impaired the country's discrete humanitarian engagement. Instead, it became the protecting power for Hungary and Bulgaria whose embassies in Santiago also hosted refugees. Austria negotiated their emigration with the Pinochet regime and continued these efforts when further persons sought refuge there in the following years.[30] In total, the Austrian Embassy served as refuge for 80, the Hungarian for 56, and the Bulgarian for 21 Chileans over the course of three years. In cooperation with the Intergovernmental Committee for European Migration (ICEM), Austria effected their emigration. In the case of emigration permits not granted for minors, Austria insisted that in the Conference on Security and Cooperation in Europe (CSCE) even the communist states of Eastern Europe had accepted the practice of family reunifications. Several other cases were highly conflicting. For example,

On Kreisky's biography, see Wolfgang Petritsch, *Bruno Kreisky. Die Biografie* (Sankt Pölten: Residenz Verlag, 2010).

27 Memo "Erich Schnacke, ex-Senator der PS; allfällige Intervention," Vienna, 13. 11. 1974, ÖStA, AdR, BMAA, II-Pol, GZ. 31.03.01/70–7/74.

28 Staribacher diaries, 14. 1. 1974.

29 Information for the Minister "Frage der Teilnahme des öst. Geschäftsträgers in Santiago de Chile an einem Festakt," Vienna, 11. 9. 1974, ÖStA, AdR, BMAA, II-Pol, GZ. 31.03.01/51–7/74.

30 Information "Neue chilenische Flüchtlinge im Gebäude der Ungarischen Botschaft in Chile," Vienna, 19. 5. 1976, Kreisky-Archiv, Chile Box 1, Mappe 1975/76.

the new Austrian Ambassador Anton Ségur-Cabanac (who was also criticized for his assessment of developments in Chile) refused to support the emigration of a refugee convicted of murder (whether the underlying motives were political was disputed) and favored his surrender to the Chilean authorities. After heated debates, he was replaced by Chargé d'Affaires Manfred Kiepach who eventually succeeded in getting the sentence converted into an expulsion from the country. The refugee and his family arrived in Vienna in November 1976. By the end of the year, Austria had accepted 313 refugees from Chile and thus "quite considerably exceeded" the original 200-person quota.[31]

Chileans found refuge not only in Latin American and Western countries but also in several communist states. Some of them were unsatisfied with their situation and actively searching for a "better country of asylum," but usually to no avail. The UNHCR stressed that it "is not a travel agency." AI feared their deportation to Chile and only in this case Austria would have been willing to take them.[32] This applied specifically to Argentina after the military coup of 1976 as well.

Argentina was an important refuge for Chileans, Uruguayans, and Paraguayans who had fled their countries. After the coup, the Austrian government reacted to appeals by AI and other NGOs and quickly declared its willingness to receive 250 refugees from Argentina.[33] The embassy in Buenos Aires continuously intervened in favor of emigration permits. With the arrival of Chilean and Uruguayan refugees from Argentina and further family reunifications, the government considered "the current Austrian Chile action as completed."[34] In the future only, "special cases that are particularly worthy of consideration" should be admitted. Indeed, they kept increasing the number of Chilean refugees in Austria into the 1980s, reaching approximately 1,500.[35] The more restrictive

---

31 Memo "Menschenrechte in Chile. Ersuchen des GS der VN um Information," Vienna, 29.6. 1977, ÖStA, AdR, BMAA, II-Pol, GZ. 31.03.00/23-II.1/77. For a detailed documentation, see folder "Segur-Cabanac," Kreisky-Archiv, Chile Box 2.
32 Memo "Chileflüchtlinge; Einreise aus der Schweiz nach Österreich," Vienna, 22.11.1974; and memo "Chile-Flüchtlinge; Einreise aus der Schweiz nach Österreich," BMI, Zl. 8556/50-SL/IV/ 74, Vienna, 30.10.1974; and Notiz, 12.12.[1974], Kreisky-Archiv, Chile Box 1, Mappe 1974.
33 Memo "Argentinien: Appell von Amnesty International zur Aufnahme von Flüchtlingen," Vienna, 3.8.1976, ÖStA, AdR, BMAA, II-Pol, GZ. 8.03.01/14-II.1/76; Memo "'Arbeitsgruppe Sozialisten für Chile'; politisch verfolgte Chilenen in Argentinien," Vienna, 23.9.1976, ÖStA, AdR, BMAA, II-Pol, GZ. 8.03.01/17-II.1/76.
34 Memo "Menschenrechte in Chile. Ersuchen des GS der VN um Information," Vienna, 29.6. 1977, ÖStA, AdR, BMAA, II-Pol, GZ. 31.03.00/23-II.1/77.
35 Memo "Auswirkungen der Generalamnestie in Chile; weitere Gewährung des politischen Asyls in Österreich," Vienna, 14.7.1978, ÖStA, AdR, BMAA, II-Pol, GZ. 31.03.00/26-II.1/78; Memo "Asylwerber aus Argentinien; Überschreitung des Kontingentes für die Aufnahme in Österreich," Viennna, 7.6.1978, ÖStA, AdR, BMAA, II-Pol, GZ. 8.07.01/3-II.1/78.

admission practice was justified with the limited funds available and "difficulties with the integration of Latin American refugees in Austria."[36]

The acceptance of Chilean refugees, representing a varied sample of the country's left, reversed the predominant pattern of welcoming refugees from communism. Interpretations of their reception in Austria clash between activists and officials. Activists from the Austrian "Chile Solidarity Front" blamed the Austrian authorities for how they had dealt with the refugees.[37] Former officials claim to have done everything according to the national and international standards of the time and saw no reason for privileging refugees who in their view behaved predominantly like exile politicians.[38] One example would be the accommodation of refugees. While several refugees expected to be placed in something like a hotel but not in a camp and if so, not for long, Austrian officials stressed the cost of constructing apartments for them. The houses built originally for Ugandan Asians were named "Macondo" by activists and refugees, who, among other things, criticized their remote location. A detailed discussion of the various discrepancies in expectations, experiences, and perceptions of officials, activists and refugees cannot be provided.[39] What matters are the limits and possibilities of activists and NGOs in influencing politics.

While the refugees' initial hopes for a quick return to Chile faded over the years, the "Chile Solidarity Front" stayed active and continued to criticize the Austrian government for its relations with Chile and similar regimes.[40] Echoing AI's request to the World Bank to deny the junta fresh loans, the "Chile Solidarity Front" complained about the increasing trade volume between Austria and Chile. The foreign ministry opposed sanctions not only because opposition voices from Chile also held the view that an economic boycott would primarily harm the population but also because it would impair Austrian economic interests.[41] Calls to sever diplomatic relations with Chile never subsided, but Kreisky kept his stance. Replying to petitioners, he listed Austria's merits in the refugee sector, integration efforts and related costs, interventions for emigration permits, and ongoing family reunification processes. He concluded by stressing his conviction that all this "would be largely impracticable if Austria severed relations."[42] Internally, Kreisky stated that "the Left" had to make a decision about its politics

---

36 Memo "Asylwerber aus Argentinien; Überschreitung des Kontingentes für die Aufnahme in Österreich," Vienna, 7.6.1978, ÖStA, AdR, BMAA, II-Pol, GZ. 8.07.01/3-II.1/78.

37 Berger (eds.), *Zerstörte Hoffnung, gerettetes Leben.*

38 Stanek, *Verfolgt Verjagt Vertrieben*, 112–132.

39 For the diverging perspectives, cf. ibid. and Berger, *Solidarität mit Chile.*

40 Ibid.

41 Memo "Wirtschaftssanktionen gegen Chile?," Vienna, 23.2.1976, ÖStA, AdR, BMAA, II-Pol, GZ. 31.20.01/1-II.1/76.

42 Kreisky to Seitner, Vienna, 13.12.1977, Kreisky-Archiv, Chile Box 1, Mappe 1977.

regarding Chile: "You can either negotiate with the regime to get details or constantly humiliate them and then you will get nothing."[43]

Similar to the dialogue with Eastern Europe, in its contacts with Latin American politicians, Austria emphasized that it did not regard human rights as a political means but as support for individuals, referring to the many humanitarian cases solved in Eastern Europe and Chile. Visiting Argentina in 1979, Foreign Minister Willibald Pahr handed over a list of eleven human rights cases in which Austria had been engaged for quite some time. As in the case of dialogue with Eastern European politicians, he declared that Austria did not intend to interfere in the internal affairs of Argentina but had a humanitarian interest in the emigration of these individuals to Austria.[44] By the late 1970s, Austria's human rights politics toward Latin America did not differ from the approach taken in Eastern Europe. "Silent diplomacy" prevailed and economic relations developed. As in the case of Eastern Europe, Austria opposed isolating regimes, whether it be Chile or Cuba. The example of Nicaragua showcased how much Austria's attitude toward Latin America had changed and to what degree interest had increased throughout the 1970s. Already in 1978, a "solidarity committee" was formed and chaired by Kreisky himself. Austrian support aimed at assisting a desired democratic "third way," serving as a counterexample to military and communist dictatorships.[45] However, idealistic foreign policy aims continued to conflict with economic interests (most notably in the nationalized industries that had secured full employment in Austria for most of the 1970s and were on the road to a severe crisis in the early 1980s).

In the aftermath of the coup, Kreisky had decided against selling machine guns to Chile.[46] However, this stance on the export of weaponry had already weakened by the mid-1970s.[47] In 1980, a weapons-manufacturing enterprise in Austria's nationalized industries concluded a 162 million USD deal to export tanks and machine guns to Chile. This happened with the full backing of the government, and Kreisky justified his approval by referring to a contract clause "guaranteeing" that the delivered "machines" would be used for defensive pur-

43 Staribacher diaries, 20.2.1978.
44 Memcon Pahr – Pastor, 11.9.1979, ÖStA, AdR, BMAA, II-Pol, GZ. 518.02.02/106-II.1/79.
45 Memcon Pahr – Van der Klaauw, 11.6.1980, ÖStA, AdR, BMAA, II-Pol, GZ. 518.02.02/27-II.1/80. On Austria and Nicaragua, see Laurin Blecha, "Von Ottakring nach Cuatro Esquinas. Beziehungen und Kooperationen zwischen Nicaragua und Österreich von 1979 bis 1990," in *Kleinstaaten und sekundäre Akteure im Kalten Krieg. Politische, wirtschaftliche, militärische und kulturelle Wechselbeziehungen zwischen Europa und Lateinamerika*, edited by Albert Manke and Kateřina Březinová (Bielefeld: transcript, 2016), 275–302.
46 Memo "Ausfuhr von Maschinenpistolen nach Chile," Vienna, 9.9.1975, ÖStA, AdR, BMAA, II-Pol, GZ. 505.02.00/165-II.1/75.
47 Memo "Fa. Hirtenberger; Antrag auf Ausfuhr von 10 Mio. Zündhütchen für Militärpatronen nach Chile," Vienna, 13.4.1976, ÖStA, AdR, BMAA, II-Pol, GZ. 31.05.80/1-II.1/76.

poses only. The insignificance of such a guarantee by Pinochet's regime caused public outrage – not least because tanks manufactured in Austria were used during the coup in Bolivia in July 1980. After heated debates, in which the significance of such exports for the Austrian job market surfaced prominently, a broadening protest coalition of activists and refugees filing petitions, organizing demonstrations, and even conducting hunger strikes, finally achieved a reversal of the course and the export deal was called off in August.[48] This episode serves as a reminder that human rights policies conflicted with other, often economic, interests and undermined Austria's reputation in the field domestically and internationally. Chile was of "symbolic character,"[49] and for years, debates about relations and economic dealings with the country remained highly emotional.[50] Kreisky was criticized for meeting the Chilean minister of economics in 1982, whom he told that for Austria, as a country at the demarcation line of two political systems, it was indispensable to maintain economic relations regardless of political systems, stressing that "no one will prevent us from doing so." When their exchange moved on to Chile's role as a country of immigration, Kreisky raised the issue of Polish refugees in Austria and recommended his interlocutor to consider taking some of them.[51] Seemingly, he considered the refugee producing country a safe haven for refugees who had fled a communist regime.

Indochinese Refugees in Austria: From Small Quotas to Solidarity with the "Boat People"

The Vietnam War had created different and changing emotions in Austria. In comparison to other Western countries (most notably neutral Sweden), protest against the Vietnam War in Austria was relatively small. Despite advocating for peace in Indochina, Austrian politicians refrained from criticizing the USA. While diplomatic relations with South Vietnam were never intense, they had only been established with North Vietnam in late 1972.[52] After the Paris Peace Accords of January 1973, the "Austrian National Committee – Vietnam Aid" was formed.

---

48 Berger, *Solidarität mit Chile*, 89–95; Thomas Riegler, "'Macht's es unter der Tuchent'. Die Waffengeschäfte der österreichischen Verstaatlichten Industrie und der Noricum-Skandal," *Vierteljahrshefte für Zeitgeschichte* 64 (2016) 1: 99–137.
49 Staribacher diaries, 20.8.1980.
50 Staribacher diaries, 10.11.1981.
51 Memcon "Besuch des chilenischen Wirtschaftsministers beim Herrn Bundeskanzler," Vienna, 28.6.1982, Kreisky-Archiv, Chile Box 2, Mappe 1982.
52 Wolfgang Mueller and Maximilian Graf, "An Austrian mediation in Vietnam? The superpowers, neutrality, and Kurt Waldheim's good offices," in *Neutrality and Neutralism in the Global Cold War. Between or within the blocs?* edited by Sandra Bott et al. (London: Routledge, 2016), 127–143.

It consisted of more than 40 Austrian NGOs and funded aid projects in North and South Vietnam, Laos, and Kampuchea. The government tripled the donations collected by the committee resulting in a total amount of more than 40 million Austrian Schillings (ATS). With the victory of the Vietcong in spring 1975, the future of many aid projects seemed insecure,[53] and Kreisky was in favor of a conversion of the available 5.2 million ATS to refugee aid.[54] Diplomats doubted whether the committee would be able to reasonably distribute aid "under such chaotic conditions."[55] The Austrian Red Cross sent drugs worth almost half a million ATS to Vietnam.[56] In reaction to various international appeals, the Austrian government decided to support the work of the UNHCR and the International Committee of the Red Cross in Vietnam with 2 million ATS. This meager sum in international comparison was explicitly understood as "in addition" to the 28.7 million ATS provided when tripling the donations collected by the committee.[57]

However, money alone did not solve the refugee crisis in Indochina. The U.S. withdrawal and the establishment of communist rule in the South, with all its hardships, such as terror in re-education camps and the severe economic consequences of collectivization, set in motion a mass exodus of hundreds of thousands. Even before the fall of Saigon, Austrian diplomats pointed to the worsening refugee situation in Vietnam. The Austrian ambassador in Bangkok spoke of "apocalyptic dimensions."[58] At the Austrian Foreign Ministry, the U.S. ambassador spoke of a "tragedy of enormous proportions," detailing refugee admission to the United States and his government's appeal to all countries: "The United States government hopes that each country will accept at least 100 refugees, but it also recognizes that if a country's economic situation does not allow it to accept poor refugees, it could accept refugees with vocational training." The

---

53 Memo "UNHCR; Hilfsprogramm für die Flüchtlinge in Indochina für die Periode 1974 bis 1975," Vienna, 6.2.1975, ÖStA, AdR, BMAA, II-Pol, GZ. 234.19.08/1-II.4/75; Memo "Vereinte Nationen: Hilfsaktion für Vietnam," Vienna, 27.7.1976, ÖStA, AdR, BMAA, II-Pol, GZ. 234. 03.03/3-II.3/76.

54 Memo "Österreichische Flüchtlingshilfe in Südvietnam und Kambodscha; Appell des Generalsekretärs der Vereinten Nationen und des IKRK," Vienna, 4.4.1975, ÖStA, AdR, BMAA, II-Pol, GZ. 234.19.01/1-II.4/75; Information for the Chancellor, State secretary Elfriede Karl, Vienna, 22.4.1975, Kreisky-Archiv, Box Vietnam; Staribacher diaries, 22.4.1975.

55 Ambassador de Comtes to BMAA, Bangkok, 16.4.1975, ÖStA, AdR, BMAA, II-Pol, GZ. 234.19. 05/9-II.3/75.

56 Memo "Republik Vietnam; Ersuchen des südvietnamesischen Botschafters um Flüchtlingshilfe," Vienna, 21.4.1975, ÖStA, AdR, BMAA, II-Pol, GZ. 234.19.05/4-II.4/75.

57 Memo "Hilfsmassnahmen für die Flüchtlinge in Vietnam, allfälliger österreichischer Beitrag," Vienna, 11.4.1975, ÖStA, AdR, BMAA, II-Pol, GZ. 234.19.09/13-II.4/75 also see GZ. 234.19.09/ 21-II.4/75.

58 Ambassador de Comtes to BMAA, Bangkok, 16.4.1975, ÖStA, AdR, BMAA, II-Pol, GZ. 234.19. 05/8-II.3/75.

ambassador recalled Austria's role in 1956, 1968, and more recently in receiving refugees from Uganda and Chile and stressed that the United States would appreciate a positive Austrian reaction: "The number of refugees is not as important as the gesture." He expected such a step to serve as an "encouragement" for other states. The foreign ministry noted that any Austrian contribution could not be "more than a gesture."[59] After an appeal by the UNHCR, Austria was willing to take 100 to 200 Vietnamese or Kampuchean refugees.[60]

In the selection of refugees Austria aimed at finding educated people with bonds or family ties to Austria. Indeed, more than 20 refugees had named Austria as their preferred resettlement country. However, the Hong Kong authorities appealed to Austria to take unskilled bachelors and some families with members who suffered from tuberculosis and were thus not eligible for admission in the USA or Canada. Hence, the consulate aimed "to reserve at least a certain amount of restraint in the selection of refugees in order to avoid that a large number of people who cannot find admission in other countries for health or other reasons are deported to Austria."[61] When asked to admit more refugees, Vienna explained that Austria regarded itself primarily as a first asylum country that had "to accept a large number of refugees on an ongoing basis." Additionally, the "particularly difficult" and costly integration of "refugees from overseas" was stressed.[62]

The increasing numbers of "boat people" arriving on the Thai and Malay coasts and their desperate situation required further international action. The Austrian Embassy in Bangkok reported: "The conditions on board the ships are mostly desolate due to overcrowding, food and water are scarce, and children were born on some boats during the voyage. The plight of these boat refugees is exacerbated by the fact that no country allows them to go ashore where they would have to be housed in refugee camps, which would make the country of

---

59 Memo "Aufnahme von Vietnamflüchtlingen," Vienna, 28.4.1975, ÖStA, AdR, BMAA, II-Pol, GZ. 234.19.13/4-II/1/75.

60 Memo "Aufnahme von vietnamesischen bzw. kambodschanischen Flüchtlingen durch Österreich," Vienna, 26.5.1975, ÖStA, AdR, BMAA, II-Pol, GZ. 234.19.13/13-II.4/75; Information for the Chancellor and the Minister of the Interior "Ersuchen des UN-Flüchtlingshochkommissärs betreffend Aufnahme von vietnamesischen bzw. kambodschanischen Flüchtlingen durch Österreich," Vienna, 12.5.1975, ÖStA, AdR, BMAA, II-Pol, GZ. 234.19.13/9-II.1/75.

61 Consul general Peterlik to BMAA, Hong Kong, 20.6.1975, ÖStA, AdR, BMAA, II-Pol, GZ. 234.19.13/30-II.4/75; Peterlik to BMAA, Hong Kong, 15.5.1975, ÖStA, AdR, BMAA, II-Pol, GZ. 234.19.13/14-II.4/75; Peterlik to BMAA, Hong Kong, 16.5.1975, ÖStA, AdR, BMAA, II-Pol, GZ. 234.19.13/15-II.4/75.

62 Memo "Indochinahilfe der Vereinten Nationen; derzeitiger Stand der Beitragsleistungen," Vienna, 30.6.1975, ÖStA, AdR, BMAA, II-Pol, GZ. 234.19.08/31-II.4/75; Memo "UNHCR; Aktionen zugunsten von Flüchtlingen ('displaced persons') aus Indochina," Vienna, 25.2.1976, ÖStA, AdR, BMAA, II-Pol, GZ. 234.19.13/5-II.4/76.

asylum responsible. The local authorities, therefore, prefer to provide the refugees with food and water and send them back to the high seas." Even though Austria held the view that it had "already made a very significant contribution to solving the refugee problem in relation to the size of the country,"[63] the Austrian Embassy in Kuala Lumpur stressed that additional admissions "would make it easier for the Malaysian government to maintain its previous, relatively positive humanitarian stance." It was the same "international solidarity" that Austria expected when facing a refugee crisis.[64] Faced with a corresponding appeal by the UNHCR, the foreign ministry opined that "for reasons of appearance" Austria should grant asylum to "a smaller number of additional Indochinese refugees." After some resistance (justified with the recent admissions from Argentina, lack of accommodation and limited financial resources),[65] the ministry of the interior announced that Austria would accept a maximum of 20 additional people.[66] The UNHCR was informed that "it would be desirable to put this group of refugees together in such a way that their integration does not result in additional and avoidable difficulties."[67] The subsequent "dry spell" in further admissions[68] was not overcome by petitions and appeals to Kreisky by individuals and groups in civil society as well as NGOs. In his replies, the chancellor referred to the exhaustion of quotas and stressed that only family reunifications in direct line (parents-children) were possible at the moment. The ministry of the interior argued: "A breach of this practice would likely trigger a new wave of entry requests from Vietnamese and Cambodian refugees, which would far exceed the quota set by the federal government at the time."[69] Obviously, the ministry believed that the admission of additional refugees would constitute a pull factor of global proportions.

---

63 Embassy Bangkok to BMAA, 29.7.1976, ÖStA, AdR, BMAA, II-Pol, GZ. 234.19.13/15-II.4/76; Memo "Flüchtlinge aus Vietnam; Intervention des Vertreters des UNHCR," Vienna, 8.9.1976, ÖStA, AdR, BMAA, II-Pol, GZ. 234.19.13/20-II.4/76.

64 Ambassador Ziegler to BMAA, Kuala Lumpur, 29.9.1976, ÖStA, AdR, BMAA, II-Pol, GZ. 234.19.13/23-II.4/76.

65 Memo "Asylwerber aus Vietnam; Ersuchen um weitere Aufnahme," Vienna, 25.8.1976, ÖStA, AdR, BMAA, II-Pol, GZ. 234.19.13/17-II.4/76; Memo "Asylwerber aus Vietnam; Ansuchen des UNHCR um weitere Aufnahme von Flüchtlingen," Vienna, 15.9.1976, ÖStA, AdR, BMAA, II-Pol, GZ. 234.19.13/21-II.4/76.

66 Memo "UNHCR; Hilfsprogramm für indochinesische Flüchtlinge ('boat people')," Vienna, 5.11.1976, ÖStA, AdR, BMAA, II-Pol, GZ. 234.19.13/27-II.4/76.

67 Representation Geneva to BMAA, 5.11.1976, ÖStA, AdR, BMAA, II-Pol, GZ. 234.19.13/32-II.4/76.

68 Memo "UNHCR; Sonderprogramm für Indochina," Vienna, 19.1.1977, ÖStA, AdR, BMAA, II-Pol, GZ. 234.03.03/2-II.4/77; Memo "UNHCR; Sonderprogramm für Thailand," Vienna, 18.3.1977, ÖStA, AdR, BMAA, II-Pol, GZ. 234.03.03/4-II.4/77.

69 Information for the Minister, Vienna, 27.5.1977, BMI, Zl. 18.795/89-II/6/77, Kreisky-Archiv, Box Vietnam.

Upon their arrival, refugees were immediately supplied with proper clothing and underwent a medical examination. Language classes were held in the camps, and the authorities sought to get the refugees into occupations. Some refugees were granted university stipends. By the end of 1976, a total of 77 asylum seekers were provided with 26 apartments and more were being made available. There was a strong impetus to "integrate" those who were still in camps by getting them housing and jobs.[70] As a result of previous experience, the ministry of the interior held the view that refugees from "a different cultural area" and with "a different mentality" would need time to become accustomated to the new environment and "only through integration into job processes and the needs of daily life [...] indirectly [be] forced to learn the German language." Controversies surrounding the treatment of Indochinese refugees in Austria seem to have been similar to the Chilean case. For example, Kreisky received a letter complaining that the staff at Camp Thalheim treated refugees primarily as an annoyance. Specific accusations concerned the occupancy of rooms, the absence of language classes, water and electricity rationing, and the cancellation of pocket money for a group of refugees. As in the case of the complaints by Chilean refugees, the ministry of the interior produced a detailed statement refuting the accusations. It denied the complaints regarding occupancy and language classes. The rationing was explained as a justified consequence of unacceptable waste of electricity and water. The cut of pocket money was labelled an "educational measure on the part of the camp management," for refugees who while drunk had broken five windows, caused further damage and threatened a doctor, requiring police intervention. Furthermore, the ministry stressed that many of the staff members had been refugees themselves and "look back on decades of experience with asylum seekers of various nationalities and social classes."[71] Be that as it may, the episode gives us a revealing glance at the authorities' experience with the refugees and we can see a pattern of conflicting views with which observers of current events should be familiar.

The share of Vietnamese refugees of Chinese descent had always been high but their number escalated significantly when tensions between Vietnam and China were aggravated and finally led to war in early 1979. In 1978, the Austrian Consulate in Hong Kong sent an alarming report to Vienna about the increasing numbers of refugees "coming to Hong Kong in boats or as shipwrecked people" and concluded: "All the signs seem to indicate that Vietnam is making no move to

---

70 Information for the Minister, Vienna, 5. 11. 1976, BMI, Zl. 16.000/86-IV/5/1976, Kreisky-Archiv, Box Vietnam.

71 Information for the Minister, Vienna, 27. 7. 1979, BMI, Zl. 1.240/36-IV/5/79, Kreisky-Archiv, Box Vietnam.

stop the Chinese exodus."[72] The number of "boat people" quadrupled from 15,000 in 1977 to 62,000 in 1978. In summer 1979, a total of 200,000 had already reached the coasts of neighboring states in the South China Sea and international media coverage of their fate emotionally moved Europeans. A study on the reception of the "boat people," comparable with Frank Bösch's landmark article on Germany,[73] has yet to be written. The following paragraphs provide first insights into the Austrian scenario. The precarious situation of these refugees and the global attention they received, caused Kreisky to urge his government to act. After a lengthy discussion, the ministers agreed on the admission of 100 families.[74] It was estimated that this would equal a total number of 300 to 400 refugees. In face of the drama of the "boat people," individuals and organizations had offered the government help with their reception and care. From this, a new approach resulted: "The greater the number of such private aid offers, the higher the number of Vietnamese refugees admitted to Austria will be."[75]

The engagement of society reached new dimensions. In letters to Kreisky, some people compared the situation in Vietnam with the Holocaust and spoke of Austrian responsibility. Others developed ideas about how to increase donations and proposed that Austrian families could foster child refugees. While some correspondents expressed their gratitude for the additional admissions, others referred to higher quotas offered by countries such as Switzerland and qualified the Austrian numbers as "alibi action."[76] Politicians were fully aware that "our numbers are really not even a drop in the ocean."[77] Basically, Austria remained "convinced that regional refugee problems can best be solved regionally." Offering refugees from the Global South a "permanent home" thus meant providing assistance to other "countries of first asylum on other continents, which have reached the end of their ability to absorb." Kreisky regarded it a "moral obligation to provide solidarity" and expressed his hope "that the Austrian population" would "support the authorities in accommodating and integrating the newly arriving refugees."[78]

In this context the *Kuratorium für Flüchtlingshilfe* (Board of Trustees for Refugee Aid) was formed. Its purpose was to form a platform for all institutions and organizations willing to aid refugees. Propelled by the global media attention

---

72 Consul General Preissl to BMAA, Hong Kong, 11.5.1978, ÖStA, AdR, BMAA, II-Pol, GZ. 234.10.00/1-II-3/78.

73 Frank Bösch, "Engagement für Flüchtlinge. Die Aufnahme vietnamesischer "Boat People" in der Bundesrepublik," in *Zeithistorische Forschungen* 14 (2017) 1: 13–40.

74 Staribacher diaries, 4.12.1978.

75 Lennkh to Karrer et al., Vienna, 17.1.1979, Kreisky-Archiv, Box Vietnam.

76 Various letters and petitions to Kreisky, Kreisky-Archiv, Box Vietnam.

77 Staribacher diaries, 17.9.1979.

78 Letters to Kreisky and drafts of replies, Kreisky-Archiv, Box Vietnam.

for the "boat people," offerings were plenty and Austria regularly increased its quota.[79] Until late 1980, a total of 1500 additional refugees were admitted[80] and further family reunifications were negotiated with the Vietnamese authorities.[81]

A precondition for this increase were the so-called "parish partnerships" organized by the Caritas. The quotas were increased according to the binding offers made by parishes from all over the country to accommodate and care for refugees. Archbishop Cardinal Franz König set an example and hosted one Vietnamese family with three little children in the archepiscopal palace. His longtime assistant, Annemarie Fenzl remembers: "He looked after the children like a grandfather, arranged for a sandbox to be set up in the courtyard of the palace and, time and again, took them to his vacation spot in Vorarlberg." When he died in 2004, one of the kids was at his deathbed.[82] In general, the "parish partnerships" are positively remembered today and seem to have facilitated a smooth integration of the Indochinese in Austria.

Another building block of solidarity with the "boat people" was an initiative by the daily newspaper *Kurier* (supported by Kreisky) that enabled 83 Vietnamese orphans and 9 adults to be admitted to SOS Children's Villages built for this purpose. Their integration was considered almost perfect, and hence, the effort was prolonged into the 1980s.[83] Despite these success stories, the further prospects for a global Austrian refugee admissions policy were bleak.

The increased quotas for "boat people" were largely facilitated by the willingness of NGOs and civil society to accommodate these refugees and cover the costs of their integration. Additional financial contributions to the UNHCR were rejected due to the "exploding" number of refugees from Eastern Europe who were consuming available Austrian funds.[84] With the exception of 1968, their number reached a 20-year peak in 1979. Faced with exhausted reception capacities, Austria deplored the duration and selectivity of immigration procedures in the United States, Australia, and Canada, causing "long waiting periods," "uncertainty and dissatisfaction among the refugees and, as a result, a number of other problems." Once again, Austria felt overburdened and left by itself: "In view of the refugee situation in the Indochinese region, other countries often overlook the problems and costs that Austria incurs as a country of first

---

79 Embassy Bangkok to BMAA, 9.9.1980, ÖStA, AdR, BMAA, II-Pol, GZ. 233.02.40/4-II.4/80.
80 *Außenpolitischer Bericht 1980*, 161.
81 "Grundbericht über Vietnam," Beijing, 3.6.1980, ÖStA, AdR, BMAA, II-Pol, GZ. 233.16.01/1-II.3/80.
82 Michael Horowitz, "Ein Kirchenkönig als Freund der Menschen," in *Die Presse am Sonntag*, 7.2.2021, p. 16.
83 Kurier to Kreisky, Vienna, 24.10.1980, Kreisky-Archiv, Box Vietnam.
84 Memo "Das Flüchtlingsproblem im indochinesischen Raum: Die Genfer Flüchtlingskonferenz 20./21.7.1979," Kreisky-Archiv, Box USA 8.

asylum for Eastern European refugees."[85] Despite this, in 1980, Austria still felt obliged to offer a "small quota" for refugees from Cuba to "not lose its credibility as a country of asylum."[86] However, when confronted with growing numbers of refugees from Poland in 1981 (as outlined in the first section), Kreisky rejected additional quotas for Indochinese refugees as requested by AI.[87] When explaining that only family reunifications for Indochinese refugees remained possible, Austrian diplomats in Bangkok "referred to the tense situation in the refugee sector in Austria and, in particular, the slow admission of refugees from Poland by traditional immigration countries."[88]

Kreisky wrote to President Ronald Reagan calling for the admission of as many refugees as possible to the United States. He conceded that "[u]ndoubtedly, the refugee problem is much more severe in areas of crisis on other continents," but insisted "that Austria is not an immigration country and her capacity to absorb refugees therefore limited."[89] Frustrated with the slow resettlement of Polish refugees, Minister of the Interior Erwin Lanc stated: "The UN High Commissioner, who ultimately has to recognize the refugees, is very reluctant. In particular, he is determined to utilize the larger contingents of immigration countries for refugees from Vietnam. Therefore, there is hardly any room for the refugees from the East, especially for the Poles."[90]

This changed only after the imposition of martial law in Poland on 13 December 1981. Austrian appeals to the international community were beginning to show results. The United States, Canada, and Australia all agreed to accept sizable contingents of Polish refugees. Switzerland accepted 1,000 refugees, and other countries smaller contingents. Austria continued to plead for the emigration of refugees, "since Austria would not be able to take tens of thousands of refugees, due to its size and economic strength," argued foreign ministry officials, and added: "Our country can only continue its humanitarian role, if the international community will help us master this difficult task."[91] This served as an excuse for abstaining from further engagement in global refugee management. At least among Austrian diplomats, there was clear-cut preference for European refugees. During a bilateral meeting with Swiss diplomats, Ambassa-

---

85 Memo "Starkes Anwachsen des Flüchtlingsstroms nach Österreich im Jahre 1979," Kreisky-Archiv, Box USA 8.

86 Staribacher diaries, 21.4.1980.

87 Staribacher diaries, 14.7.1981.

88 Bogner to BMAA, Bangkok, 3.12.1981, ÖStA, AdR, BMAA, II-Pol, GZ. 233.02.40/2-II.4/81.

89 Kreisky to Reagan, 14.8.1981, Kreisky-Archiv, Box USA 8. On the US refugee policy of the time, see Carl J. Bon Tempo, *Americans at the Gate. The United States and Refugees during the Cold War* (Princeton: University Press, 2008), 167–196.

90 Staribacher diaries, 30.11.1981.

91 Sektion IV.2 to Sektion II, Vienna, 30.6.1982, ÖStA, AdR, BMAA, II-Pol, GZ. 166.02.40/79-II.3/82.

dor Friedrich Bauer said: "From the Austrian point of view, it must be stated that the non-European refugees, in contrast to the Eastern European refugees, can hardly be integrated. One should, therefore, strive not to lose sight of the 'European tangent' in refugee policy."[92] Despite the admission of non-European refugees in the 1970s, Austrian migration policy during the Cold War was firmly rooted in the East-West dimension. Nevertheless, the acceptance rates of asylum seekers from Eastern Europe still continued to decline. The more the Cold War drew to a close, the more this tendency became apparent.

Conclusions

Neutral Austria achieved international recognition as a humanitarian actor for its handling of the 1956 refugee crisis and successfully cultivated its role as a place of first asylum and refugee transit. Until the 1960s, Austria's engagement for the enforcement of human rights and refugee aid focused primarily on neighboring communist regimes. Thereafter, despite this manifest geographical focus, a more global approach evolved. The country's opening for asylum seekers from the Global South is one of the indicators for this development. Taking into consideration its international credibility as a refuge, Austria offered quotas for Chilean and Indochinese refugees. Although this was portrayed as a humanitarian act, the available archival sources mainly tell a story of the costs and problems related to their acceptance. In this regard (and regardless of government constellations), little has changed since then. As in recent years, non-state actors have decisively contributed to facilitating refugee reception.

In both cases, global refugee moments have triggered responses by society. The "Chile Solidarity Committee" formed after the coup was concerned not only with refugees, but also acted politically. Its engagement oscillated between unsatisfiable demands and impressive successes. Vienna's policy toward Latin American military dictatorships followed along the lines established for dealing with Eastern Europe. Dialogue was continued and aimed at improving the situation. While the much-desired loan-financed exports and other big deals for Austria's nationalized industries with the socialist states generally contributed to improving relations and, as a side effect, also facilitated the country's humanitarian efforts vis-à-vis these countries, the planned export of weapons to Chile was prevented by an activist campaign against this Austrian contribution to the junta's dark record. Austria's humanitarian engagement in the 1970s went beyond helping the victims of communism (who had shaped its development

---

92 Memcon "Beamtengespräche BMAA/EDA Botschafter Bauer, 3. Juni 1983 in Bern," ÖStA, AdR, BMAA, II-Pol, GZ. 502.16.04/24-II.1/83.

most), however, as the case of Chile shows, it was easily flawed when it conflicted with other national interests.

While protest against the Vietnam War was comparably small in Austria, people and politics soon engaged in development aid for the war-torn region. The reception of refugees from Indochina corresponded with Austria's traditional anti-communist Cold War refugee policy and its new global approach in the 1970s. The initial refugee quotas were of rather symbolic nature, but in face of the tragedy of the "boat people," a broad coalition joined forces, and Austria admitted as many refugees as society could guarantee to accommodate and care for.

Parallel to solidarity with the "boat people" and in the shadow of the reception of dissidents, the number of Eastern European refugees in Austria increased rapidly. When a steadily growing number of Poles reached Austria in 1981, this had repercussions for the country's global refugee policy. Kreisky rejected additional admissions of "boat people." Moreover, Austria saw the global response to the Indochinese refugee situation as a reason for missing quotas for Polish asylum seekers in Austria. Searching for resettlement countries, Kreisky even tried to talk Chile (for many of whose citizens Austria served as an exile location) into absorbing some of the Poles. Growing reluctance toward accepting refugees in general surfaced in the early 1980s and thus impaired the founding pillar of Austria's humanitarian engagement in the Cold War.

Furthermore, we can identify several continuities in the Austrian attitude toward non-European refugees. Among them are the supposedly greater difficulties and higher costs of their integration. Additionally, we can clearly see that the reception of refugees from the Global South did not alter the persistent focus and clear-cut preference for European refugees still manifest today. The Austrian stance that "refugee problems" are best solved regionally has not changed since the Kreisky years; nonetheless, the country's financial contributions to international on-site help have remained negligible until today. As in case of Eastern European refugees who were granted asylum in Austria, the resettlement of refugees from the Global South was primarily seen as the responsibility of "traditional immigration countries" (first and foremost the United States) who actually did not consider themselves to be such anymore. Austria self-deceivingly continued to insist that it was not a country of immigration and that a liberal asylum policy would turn into a pull factor for other migrants and refugees. Future research is bound to deepen our understanding of continuities since the 1970s and broaden our knowledge of the first receptions of non-European refugees in Austria in a multi-perspective way.

Judith Welz

In the Service of Deportation: The Development of Detention and Other Forms of Movement Restrictions in the Austrian Asylum System from 1990 to 2020

Introduction

In the late summer of 2019, Ronald Frühwirth, one of the longest-serving and best-known asylum lawyers in Austria, announced the closure of his law firm. He explained that too many of his clients had been deported to places where they were unsafe. He had lost faith in the rule of law and no longer wanted to be part of Austria's asylum system.[1] Frühwirth had begun his career some fifteen years earlier, around when the first coalition government with the conservative People's Party and the extreme right-wing Freedom Party initiated another attempt to use asylum law to reduce Austria's immigrant population.[2] In a reform process begun by Minister of the Interior Ernst Strasser in 2003 and finalized by his successor, Liese Prokop, in 2005, a number of protection standards and legal safeguards were removed, which rendered asylum claimants more vulnerable to deportation (see empirical Section 1). As a result, the comparatively liberal Asylum Act of 1997, which had been adopted to counter the most harmful effects of the previous act from 1991, was replaced by a highly restrictive version: the Asylum Act of 2005.[3] Still, history demonstrated that this was not the end but rather the continuation of restrictive asylum policy making in Austria; the act of 1997 was only an exception.

---

1 Edith Meinhardt, "Warum einer der besten Asylanwälte des Landes seine Kanzlei schließt," *Profil*, 8 August 2019 https://www.profil.at/oesterreich/roland-fruehwirth-asylanwalt-kanzlei-ende-10894507 (26 January 2022).

2 According to Kraler, this was first attempted in 1991. Albert Kraler, "The Case of Austria," in *Migration Policymaking in Europe. The Dynamics of Actors and Contexts in Past and Present* (IMISCOE Research), edited by Zincone Giovanna et al., (Amsterdam: IMISCOE Research, 2012), 36.

3 nim, "Karl Korinek: 'Da passt alles hinten und vorne nicht': Der Verfassungsgerichtshofs-Präsident übt Kritik am Fremdenrecht – Regierung müsse Fehler 'endlich reparieren'," *Der Standard*, 9 January, 2008 https://www.derstandard.at/story/3098462/karl-korinek-da-passt-alles-hinten-und-vorne-nicht (26 January 2022).

However, Austria did not always have a restrictive asylum system. In fact, before 1968, asylum was not an area of policy making at all. Since Austria was a signatory to the Geneva Refugee Convention, its principles were applicable. Successive ministers of the interior simply issued instructions to implementation officers on the ground. Larger refugee movements were collectively and generously managed; thus, Austria became the country of first entry for large numbers of refugees from Eastern Europe between 1956 and 1981. According to Patrik-Paul Volf, throughout the Cold War era, the accommodation of refugees was an important aspect of Austria's post-war nation-building process. 'The refugee from Eastern Europe' was a symbol of the country's anti-communism and alignment with Western values and a Western lifestyle.[4]

Today, Austrian officials still capitalize on Austria's image as a generous "asylum country" (German: *Asylland*) during the Cold War era but remain silent about the fact that most refugees registered in Austria between 1945 and 1981 did not remain in the country for long. Many left through resettlement programs as part of agreements and arrangements with other countries and international organizations.[5] Others transited from Austria to neighboring countries or returned to their home country after the situation there improved. Of the two million refugees who entered Austria during this time, only 650,000 remained on a long-term basis, 350,000 of which were ethnic Germans who had arrived in Austria shortly after the end of World War II.[6]

With the adoption of the first restrictive Asylum Act of 1991,[7] asylum politics finally moved from the arena of diplomacy and multilateral agreements to that of

---

4 Patrik Paul Volf, "Der politische Flüchtling als Symbol der Zweiten Republik: Zur Asyl- und Flüchtlingspolitik seit 1945," *zeitgeschichte* 22, (1995) 11–12: 415–36.

5 According to Marjoleine Zieck, Austria administered the first large-scale resettlement program with Hungarian refugees in the 1950s. Marjoleine Zieck, "The 1956 Hungarian Refugee Emergency, an Early and Instructive Case of Resettlement," *Amsterdam Law Forum* 5 (2020) 2: 45. See also Brigitta Zierer, "Willkommene Ungarnflüchtlinge 1956?," in *Asylland wider Willen: Flüchtlinge in Österreich im europäischen Kontext seit 1914*, edited by Gernot Heiss (Wien: Verl. Jugend und Volk, 1995), 166–68 (Veröffentlichungen des Ludwig-Boltzmann-Institutes für Geschichte der Gesellschaftswissenschaften 25). For more on Austria's role as a transit country for refugees, see Maximilian Graf and Sarah Knoll, "In Transit or Asylum Seekers? Austria and the Cold War Refugees from the Communist Bloc," in *Migration in Austria*, edited by Günter Bischof and Dirk Rupnow (New Orleans–Innsbruck: UNO Press; innsbruck university press 2017), 90–111 (Contemporary Austrian Studies 26).

6 Melita Sunjic, "Globale Flüchtlingstrends und die Asylsituation in Österreich." *Asylland wider Willen: Flüchtlinge in Österreich im europäischen Kontext seit 1914*, edited by Gernot Heiss (Wien: Verl. Jugend und Volk, 1995), 260 (Veröffentlichungen des Ludwig-Boltzmann-Institutes für Geschichte der Gesellschaftswissenschaften 25).

7 The Asylum Act 1991 was identified as one of the most restrictive legal frameworks concerning asylum seekers in Europe by national as well as international commentators soon. In response, civil society actors together with UNHCR founded the Gemeinsame Flüchtlingskommission (the Communitary Commission on Refugees) which held parallel, non-state asylum proce-

national policy making. Except for the Asylum Act of 1997, one government after another followed the same path by making Austrian asylum law more restrictive with each reform. These reforms were numerous; between 1991 and 2016, Austria's asylum legislation was amended twenty-nine times.[8]

Today, the extreme complexity and opaqueness of legal texts are consequences of these reforms; only a few experts and practitioners fully understand the contents of Austria's asylum system. In 2010, the president of the Austrian Administrative Court publicly stated that "asylum and migration law has already reached a degree of complexity and fogginess that requires extremely specialist knowledge by courts to solve the ambiguities and disputable cases caused by the legislative activities."[9] Legal experts Ronald Frühwirth and Ines Rössl, who analyzed reforms to the asylum law between 2003 and 2016, concluded that important rights standards for asylum seekers had been eroded in the process, especially by complicating access to the asylum procedure and legal remedy and accelerating the execution of removal decisions.[10] The current paper aims to partly unravel the complexity of these legal frameworks by exploring one particular aspect: the development of pre-removal detention and other forms of movement restrictions.

With this paper, I aim to contribute to contemporary history in the field of asylum studies. According to Dirk Rupnow, Austrian historians have largely left the study of contemporary migration and asylum to social scientists.[11] One exception is research on the so-called "guest worker era," which has produced numerous historiographic works.[12] Considerable research has also been con-

dures and issued UNHCR-protection letters which UNHCR usually only provided in countries with no functioning asylum system: Michael Genner, "Asylverfahren und Polizeistaat," in *Die Gewalt des neoliberalen Staates: Vom fordistischen Wohlfahrtsstaat zum repressiven Überwachungsstaat*, edited by Nikolaus Dimmel (Wien: facultas wuv, 2008), 434.

8 Franz Merli, "Das Aslyrecht als Experimentierfeld: Einführung," in *Das Asylrecht als Experimentierfeld: Eine Analyse seiner Besonderheiten aus vergleichender Sicht*, edited by Franz Merli and Magdalena Pöschl (Wien: Manz, 2017), 2.

9 Clemens Jabloner, "Stellungnahme des Präsidiums des VwGH. Zum Entwurf eines Bundesgesetzes, mit dem das Niederlassungs- und Aufenthaltsgesetz, das Fremdenpolizeigesetz 2005, das Asylgesetz 2005 und das Staatsbürgerschaftsgesetz 1985 geändert werden," 2011, Zl. VwGH-1706/0001-PRAES/2011, 2–3.

10 Roland Frühwirth and Ines Rössl, "Österreichs Asylpolitik. Ständiger Entzug des Zugangs zum Recht," in *Mosaik – Politik neu zusammensetzen* 2016, 15. Januar, 2016 https://mosaik -blog.at/oesterreichs-asylpolitik-staendiger-entzug-des-zugangs-zum-recht/ (27 January 2022).

11 Dirk Rupnow, "Migration," in *Österreichische Zeitgeschichte – Zeitgeschichte in Österreich: Eine Standortbestimmung in Zeiten des Umbruchs*, edited by Marcus Gräser and Dirk Rupnow (Wien, Köln: Böhlau Verlag, 2021), 247–48.

12 Verena Lorber, "To Come in to Focus: Female "Guest Workers?" from Former Yugoslavia in Austria (1960–1980)," in *Migration in Austria*, edited by Günter Bischof and Dirk Rupnow, (New Orleans, Innsbruck: UNO Press; innsbruck university press, 2017), 160–85 (Contemporary Austrian Studies 26); Christina Hollomey-Gasser, Marcel Amoser, and Gerhard

ducted on Austria's approach to refugees during the Cold War era.[13] Some works have focused on other types of migration, such as the migration of women within or outside the guest worker system or educational migration.[14] Perhaps unsurprisingly, historiographic works on the phenomena of the past thirty years are especially scarce. Exceptions include studies on the place of migration and migrants in Austrian collective memory[15] and the regulation of labor migration after "guest work."[16] By combining social science and historical approaches and

---

Hetfleisch, "Von Leerstellen, Migration und Geschlecht: Ein Werkstattbericht," in *Geschlechterverhältnisse der Migrationsgesellschaften: Repräsentationen – Kritik – Differenz*, edited by Sabine Gatt et al. (Wiesbaden: Springer VS, 2016), 95–118; Veronika Settele, "Rechtliche Grundlegungen der Arbeitsmigration nach Deutschland und Österreich in der zweiten Hälfte des 20. Jahrhunderts," in *historia.scribere* 4 (2012): 67–85, https://webapp.ui bk.ac.at/ojs2/index.php/historia_scribere/article/view/2248/1800 (28 January 2022); Hannes Wimmer (ed.), *Ausländische Arbeitskräfte in Österreich* (Frankfurt/Main: Campus-Verl., 1986).

13 Gernot Heiss (ed.), *Asylland wider Willen: Flüchtlinge in Österreich im europäischen Kontext seit 1914* (Wien: Verl. Jugend und Volk, 1995) (Veröffentlichungen des Ludwig-Boltzmann-Institutes für Geschichte der Gesellschaftswissenschaften 25); Maximilian Graf and Sarah Knoll, "Das Ende eines Mythos? Österreich und die Kommunismusflüchtlinge," in *Aufnahmeland Österreich: Über den Umgang mit Massenflucht seit dem 18. Jahrhundert*, edited by Börries Kuzmany and Rita Garstenauer (Wien: mandelbaum verlag, 2017), 206–29; Graf and Knoll, "In Transit or Asylum Seekers?". Andreas Gémes, "Deconstruction of a Myth? Austria and the Hungarian Refugees of 1956–57," https://files.iwm.at/jvfc/25_8_Gemes.pdf (28 January 2022).

14 For more on the migration of women, see for example Silvia Hahn, "Frauen – Migration," in *Frauenleben in Niederösterreich*, edited by Elisabeth Vavra Elisabeth, (Weitra, 2004, 66–68); Lorber, "Female Guest Workers?," 160–85. For more on academic migration, see Marcel Amoser in this volume. For a comprehensive discussion of Austrian contemporary history and research on migration, see Rupnow, "Migration."

15 Christiane Hintermann, "Marginalized Memories: The (In)Visibility of Migration History in Public Space in Austria," *Contemporary Austrian Studies* 26 (2017): 243–55; Dirk Rupnow, "The History and Memory of Migration in Post-War Austria: Current Trends and Future Challenges," in *Migration in Austria*, edited by Günter Bischof and Dirk Rupnow (New Orleans, Innsbruck: UNO Press; innsbruck university press, 2017), 36–65 (Contemporary Austrian Studies 26); Vida Bakondy and Renée Winter, "Schweigen und Profitieren: Überlegungen zur Fortwirkung von Strukturen nationalsozialistischer Zwangsarbeit nach 1945," in *Vom selben Schlag: Migration und Integration im niederösterreichischen Industrieviertel*, edited by Thomas Schmidinger (Wiener Neustadt: Verein Alltag-Verl., 2008), 57–64.

16 Lisa Grösel, "Die postfordistische Wende der politischen Regulation in Österreich im Bereich der Ausländer_innenpolitik: 1986 bis 1992," Diplomarbeit, Universität Wien, 2013, https://utheses.univie.ac.at/detail/23003#; 24 January 2022; Lisa Grösel, *Fremde von Staats wegen: 50 Jahre "Fremdenpolitik" in Österreich* (Wien: Mandelbaum Kritik & Utopie, 2016); Kenneth Horvath, *Die Logik der Entrechtung: Sicherheits- und Nutzendiskurse im österreichischen Migrationsregime* (Göttingen: Vandenhoeck & Ruprecht, 2014); Ilse Reiter-Zatloukal, "Ausländische Arbeitskräfte in Österreich. Die rechtsgeschichtliche Entwicklung der Arbeitsmigration seit der Frühen Neuzeit," in 100 Jahre Arbeitsmarktverwaltung. Österreich im internationalen Vergleich, edited by Mathias Krempl and Johannes Thaler (Zeitgeschichte im Kontext 12), (Göttingen: V&R unipress, 2017), 115–157.

examining the development of asylum politics after the 1990s, I aim to address some of the outlined desiderata through the current paper.

Research Design and Argument

To study a country's asylum system, one can either examine asylum seekers' rights and opportunities to achieve international protection status or focus on the state and its sovereign powers to control the inclusion and exclusion of non-nationals to and from society. In this paper, I focus on the second aspect – more specifically, how the instrument of movement restrictions has been applied in Austria over the past thirty years in the service of deportation. The research question is as follows: How have movement restrictions been used in the Austrian asylum system since the 1990s to raise the deportability of rejected asylum seekers and asylum seekers pending decision? The analyzed material primarily consists of the relevant sections from the Asylum Acts of 1991, 1997, 2003, and 2005; the Aliens Police Acts of 1954, 1994, and 2005; and their numerous reforms. Additional sources included European regulations, reports by national and international organizations, and government programs. Statistical data was derived from written parliamentary inquiries and the official homepage of the Ministry of the Interior.

Restricting mobility facilitates control and surveillance. It is unsurprising that movement restrictions and immobilization techniques have long been used as tools to increase the deportability of illegalized migrants[17] or rejected asylum seekers. The oldest, most intrusive, and – perhaps from a state's perspective – most efficient form of movement restriction is immigration detention[18] (German: *Schubhaft*). Detaining people in prisons or prison-like facilities makes their deportation relatively straightforward, as they are already in the custody of authorities when their forced removal is scheduled. Since detaining a person is, by definition, in conflict with the human right to liberty, the application of this instrument is strictly circumscribed by international legal frameworks.[19] This

---

17 According to legal scholar Tobias Klarmann, the term illegalization shifts focus from the migrant to the process, by which they acquire the status of illegality, which is why he considers it preferable to the term illegality. Tobias Klarmann, *Illegalisierte Migration. Die (De-)Konstruktion migrationsspezifischer Illegalitäten im Unionsrecht,* (Baden-Baden: Nomos, 2021) (Schriften zum Migrationsrecht 34). See also Nicholas de Genova, "Migrant 'Illegality' and Deportability in Everyday Life." *Annual Review of Anthropology,* (2002) 31: 439.

18 The term "immigration detention" is interchangeably used with "pre-removal detention" as a translation of the German term *Schubhaft.*

19 Art. 5f of the European Convention on Human Rights (Convention for the Protection of Human Rights and Fundamental Freedoms, Rome, 4.XI. 1950); Article 15 and 17 of the Directive 2008/115/EC of the European Parliament and of the Council of 16 December 2008

limitation led policy makers in many countries and at the level of the European Union (EU) to devise other forms of movement restrictions that could be applied when pre-removal detention was unavailable. In the Austrian context, these measures included other legal forms of custody, such as short-term apprehension orders (German: *Festnahmeauftrag*), detention to compel compliance (German: *Beugehaft*), or compensatory detention (German: *Ersatzfreiheitsstrafe*), and non-detention forms of mobility restrictions, including territorial movement restrictions (German: *Gebietsbeschränkung*) and orders to take residence at a specific location (German: *Anordnung zur Unterkunftnahme*) or to regularly report one's presence to authorities (German: *regelmäßige Meldeverpflichtung*). Such mobility restrictions are deemed less invasive and thus attract less political contestation than detention.

While pre-removal detention was the primary instrument used to increase the deportability of rejected asylum seekers over the first half of the study period (i. e., 1990–2005; empirical Sections 1 and 2), this study demonstrates that a more diversified and stratified approach emerged during the second half of the study period (i. e., after 2005; empirical Sections 3 and 4). First, before 2016, a system of obligations and restrictions began to replace the more repressive practice of detention in many cases. Over time, the system was gradually expanded to asylum seekers whose cases were still pending decision in the asylum procedure. Detention remained linked to the new system, as it was used when less invasive measures were not respected or proved unsuccessful. After massive migration and flight movements in 2015, pre-removal detention once again became the priority measure to facilitate deportation. Since a control system based on restrictions and obligations persisted, a large proportion of asylum seekers who have been rejected and are awaiting decision today face either detention or the permanent threat thereof.

Movement Restrictions: What the Literature Says

In nation states, non-citizens have fewer rights than citizens. One expression of this inequality is the fact that law-breaking immigrants may be punished twice for the same offense: through a sentence established in the penal code and through withdrawal of their legal residence status, an act that may ultimately lead to deportation.[20]

---

on common standards and procedures in Member States for returning illegally staying third-country nationals.

20 In Austria, non-citizens who are found guilty of a crime may be issued a "prohibition of stay" (GE: *Aufenthaltsverbot*) in addition to a criminal sentence. A prohibition of stay ends the legal

The scope of inequality and the level of violence that non-citizens are subjected to are dynamic. Before the 1990s, non-citizens were almost exclusively expelled when found guilty of a crime in Europe. Subsequently, pre-removal detention and deportation were increasingly used against non-citizens without legal residence status.[21] Some researchers have attributed this change to the transformation of the economic system from Fordism to post-Fordism, when the need for large numbers of low-skilled workers was replaced by the need for a more specialized workforce; thus, immigration became more closely regulated.[22] As a result of this paradigm shift in migration politics, which is frequently referred to as "migration management," stratified residence permit systems were established in many countries and foreign laborers were more rigorously selected according to pre-defined criteria.[23] Detention and deportation were used to exclude some non-citizens from national labor markets and to discipline those who remained in the country and worked.[24] From this perspective, economic transformation dovetailed with changing conceptions about delinquency, especially migrant delinquency.[25]

Didier Fassin coined the concept of *moral economy* to examine how perceptions of refugees have changed in Europe.[26] According to Fassin, asylum case

residence of non-citizens who hold residence status. For a discussion on the double penalty in other countries, see Christin Achermann, "Excluding the Unwanted: Dealing with Foreign-National Offenders in Switzerland," in *Politik der Inklusion und Exklusion*, edited by Ilker Ataç and Sieglinde Rosenberger (Göttingen–Wien: V & R unipress; Vienna University Press, 2013), 91–110 (Migrations- und Integrationsforschung 4); Melanie Griffiths. "Foreign, Criminal: A Doubly Damned Modern British Folk-Devil." *Citizenship Studies* 21 (2017) 5: 527–46; Pierre Tevanian, "Die Doppelbestrafung ist eine mentale Struktur," in *Das große Gefängnis*, edited by Birgit Mennel and Monika Mokre (Wien-Linz-Berlin-London-Zürich: transversal texts, 2015), 69–70.

21 Daniel Kanstroom refers to the former type as post-entry social control, to the latter as extended border control. Daniel Kanstroom, "Deportation, Social Control, and Punishment: Some Thoughts About Why Hard Laws Make Bad Cases." *Harvard Law Review* 113 (2000) 8: 1906–1914.

22 Birgit Mennel and Monika Mokre, "Zu diesem Buch," in *Das große Gefängnis*, edited by Birgit Mennel and Monika Mokre (Wien-Linz-Berlin-London-Zürich: transversal texts, 2015), 18–19.

23 In Austria, the paradigm shift is reflected in the adoption of the Residence Act of 1992, which introduced a system of various residence titles with different social and labor market rights attached to them: Ataç, Ilker, and Albert Kraler. "Gewünschte, Geduldete und Unerwünschte: Klassifizieren, Selektieren, Stratifizieren. Migrationspolitik als Strategie des Filterns," *MALMOE*, no. 33 (2006): 25–26.

24 Nicholas de Genova, "Spectacles of Migrant 'Illegality': The Scene of Exclusion, the Obscene of Inclusion." *Ethnic and Racial Studies* 36 (2013) 7: 1188.

25 Mennel and Mokre, "Zu diesem Buch," 18–19.

26 According to Didier Fassin, the moral economy refers to the "production, circulation and appropriation of norms and obligations, values and affects taking place with regard to specific societal problems at a given moment in time" (*author's translation*). Didier Fassin, "Vom Rechtsanspruch *zum* Gunsterweis: Zur moralischen Ökonomie der Asylvergabepraxis im

workers generously applied relevant legal frameworks until the early 1970s, when there was a high need for a foreign work force. This changed with the oil crisis, when society's growing reluctance to the integration of foreigners was translated into suspicion about refugees' narratives among case workers. Consequences included a considerable decrease in recognition rate of refugees, leading to higher rates of detention and deportation. Changes in the moral economy meant that this approach to law enforcement was not only tolerated but deemed necessary by a majority of society and state personnel.[27]

Scholarly interest in contemporary forms of immigration detention is relatively recent. However, since the turn of the century, a considerable body of literature has emerged.[28] Researchers have discussed immigration detention and its role in border control in the context of the growing criminalization of migrants[29] from the perspective of detainees and authorities' experiences[30] and through the lens of resistance practices.[31]

Lately, research has expanded to other forms of movement restrictions that have become part of the arsenal of border control. Daniel Fisher, Andrew Burridge, and Nick Gill found that measures such as regular reporting obligations to police or residence orders in the United Kingdom restrict the mobility of the concerned and facilitate their observation and policing to an extent that is comparable to detention. Hence, the researchers suggested the "carceral to be

---

heutigen Europa," *Mittelweg 36. Zeitschrift des Hamburger Instituts für Sozialforschung* 25 (2016) 1: 65 https://www.eurozine.com/vom-rechtsanspruch-zum-gunsterweis/?pdf (24 January 2022).

27 Ibid., 64–70.

28 Mary Bosworth and Sarah Turnbull, "Immigration Detention, Punishment, and the Criminalization of Migration," *Criminal Justice, Borders and Citizenship Research Paper*, 2014, 1.

29 Alessandro de Giorgi, "Immigration Control, Post-Fordism, and Less Eligibility", *Punishment & Society* 12 2 (2010): 147–67; Juliet Stumpf, "The Crimmigration Crisis: Immigrants, Crime, and Sovereign Power," *American University Law Review* 56 (2006) 2: 368–418; Nicholas de Genova, "The Production of Culprits: From Deportability to Detainability in the Aftermath of "Homeland Security"," *Citizenship Studies* 11 (2007) 5: 421–48.

30 Mary Bosworth, *Inside Immigration Detention* (Oxford: Oxford University Press, 2014). Mary Bosworth, "Immigration Detention, Punishment and the Transformation of Justice," *Social & Legal Studies* 28 1 (2019) 1: 81–99; Francesca Esposito et al. "Ecology of Sites of Confinement: Everyday Life in a Detention Center for Illegalized Non-Citizens." *American journal of community psychology* 63, 1–2 (2019): 190–207.

31 Peter Nyers, "Abject Cosmopolitanism. The Politics of Protection in the Anti-Deportation Movement," in *The Deportation Regime. Sovereignty, Space, and the Freedom of Movement*, edited by Nicholas de Genova and Nathalie Peutz, (Durham: Duke University Press, 2010), 413–42; Antje Ellermann, "Undocumented Migrants and Resistance in the Liberal State," *Politics & Society* 38 (2010) 3: 408–429; JoAnn McGregor, "Contestations and consequences of deportability: hunger strikes and the political agency of non-citizens", *Citizenship Studies* 15 (2011) 5: 597–611.

gradient rather than binary."[32] Similarly, Leanne Weber and Sharon Pickering questioned the perception that non-detention types of movement restrictions are less invasive than detention. By considerably reducing opportunities and options and constructing an impasse, they restrict the lives of the concerned to the extent that they are frequently driven to turn themselves in for "voluntary returns."[33] According to the researchers, measures called "non-invasive" by officials are often designed to align actions and behaviors with the state's "border management goals" and to prevent the expenses associated with more repressive techniques.[34]

The Contours of Asylum Seekers' Detainability Today

Asylum seekers in Austria are granted preliminary authorization to remain in the country for the duration of the asylum procedure. Therefore, they may neither be detained nor deported. If a case is decided against, asylum case workers assess whether a person's removal would constitute a breach of Articles 2, 3, or 8 of the European Convention of Human Rights (ECHR). Articles 2 and 3 forbid a person's deportation if their life would be at risk or if they would face torture or other forms of inhumane or degrading treatment or punishment in the country that they would be returned to. Article 8 protects an individual's private and family life and allows deportation only if the state's interests in a particular deportation case carry greater weight than an individual's interests in remaining in the country. If no obstacles to the removal of a rejected asylum seeker are found, they may be issued a removal decision (German: *Ausweisungsentscheidung*). In most cases, this decision entails an invitation to autonomously leave the country. A person becomes deportable only if they are still in the country after this deadline.

Pre-removal detention is defined as an administrative measure to facilitate deportation. Since any form of arrest conflicts with personal liberties, pre-removal detention is tightly circumscribed by international and human rights law. According to the most important principles, it should be considered a measure of last resort, upheld for the shortest possible period of time, and proportional.

In the following sections, I analyze how pre-removal detention and other forms of movement restrictions have been developed and refined in the context

---

32 Daniel X.O. Fisher et al., "The political mobilities of reporting: tethering, slickness and asylum control", *Mobilities* 14 (2019) 5: 635.
33 Leanne Weber and Sharon Pickering, "Constructing Voluntarism: Technologies of 'intent management' in Australian Border Controls", in *New Border and Citizenship Politics,* edited by Helen Schwenken and Sabine Ruß-Sattar (London: Palgrave Macmillan, 2014), 23.
34 Ibid., 16–18, 25–28.

of the Austrian asylum regime since the 1990s to increase the effectiveness of deportation.

The Development of Pre-Removal Detention and Other Forms of Movement Restrictions in the Austrian Asylum System Since the 1990s

1.   1990s: The Beginnings of Pre-Removal Detention for Asylum Seekers

As previously mentioned, incarceration conflicts with the universal right to liberty. The ECHR legitimized the detention of non-citizens as early as 1950 by adding an exception to this right; it states that "a person against whom action is being taken with a view to deportation or extradition"[35] may be lawfully detained. While this clause laid the foundations of immigration detention, it also limited its use to cases in which state agents conducted concrete activities that were directed at removing a person. Once a removal becomes implausible, the person must be freed. At the Austrian national level, immigration detention has been regulated according to the ECHR since 1954.[36]

Despite the long-standing availability of pre-removal detention, asylum seekers were rarely detained in Austria before 1990 because few were denied status and those who were could easily legalize their stay by obtaining employment. At the time, the principle that non-citizens were generally "entitled to take residence in Austria for an unlimited period of time" as established in the second paragraph of the Aliens Police Act of 1954 was valid.

The situation changed in 1990 following a shift in attitudes toward refugees. According to Peter Zuser, the dominant discourse that spurred this change was mainly disseminated by Minister of the Interior Franz Löschnak and other high-ranking bureaucrats and members of the Social Democrats. They portrayed asylum seekers as immigrants in disguise who used the asylum system to attain legal residence without truly facing persecution in their countries of origin.[37] The threat of "the economic refugee" created an opportunity for the political lead-

---

35 Art. 5f of the ECHR.

36 Ilse Reiter-Zatloukal, ""… ein äußerst gefährliches Subjekt"! Zur Rechtsgeschichte des österreichischen Ausweisungsrechts," in *Vom Umgang mit den "Anderen". Historische und menschenrechtliche Perspektiven der Abschiebung*, edited by Manfred Nowak and Edith Saurer (Wien: NWV – Neuer Wiss. Verl., 2013), 82 (Studienreihe des Ludwig-Boltzmann-Instituts für Menschenrechte 25).

37 Peter Zuser, "Die Konstruktion der Ausländerfrage in Österreich. Eine Analyse des öffentlichen Diskurses 1990" in IHS Political Science Series, Working Paper 35 https://irihs.ihs.ac.a t/id/eprint/916/1/pw_35.pdf (23 January 2022).

ership to promote several policy changes related to migration and asylum politics that had already been pressing before the new immigration movement reached Austria, which were due to impending EU membership and changing labor market needs. In response, a legal amendment was passed in early 1990 to remove the general right to legal residence and replaced it with a requirement to apply for it. Consequently, anyone who was unsuccessful in the application process would be illegalized. The existing instrument of pushbacks was expanded in scope, and a new instrument, administrative removal, was established to enable police to act against those who were illegally present in Austria.

Due to the change in attitudes toward refugees, the asylum authorities' decision-making practices also changed. In 1980, 71.6% of asylum applicants (5,127 out of 7,159 decisions) were granted refugee status; however, this rate declined to 6.8% ten years later (864 out of 12,648 decisions).[38] It is important to note that the largest group of refugees who settled in Austria in the 1990s were exempt from the asylum procedure. Around 93,000 refugees from former Yugoslavia were accommodated as de facto refugees and given temporary residence status rather than refugee status.[39]

With the new laws in place, rejected asylum seekers figured for the first time among pre-removal detainees in Austrian prisons. Since the Austrian immigration detention structure lacked a functioning system of control and accountability, some police departments developed practices that went far beyond the bounds of legal permissibility. Frequently, asylum seekers were detained right after filing their application. In the official notification, police explained the detention by the fact that they had illegally crossed into Austria Police even though asylum seekers were legally protected from deportation and consequently from detention for the duration of the asylum procedure.[40] As a care system for people in deportation-related detention (German: *Schubhaftbetreuung*) had yet to be established, asylum seekers were often left to fight their cases alone. Since language skills, legal knowledge, and financial means were often scarce, they were often unsuccessful. Moreover, the Ministry of the Interior, which functioned as the appeal body at the time, usually upheld the first decision on the rare occasions that an appeal process was initiated. The fact that Austria lacked an independent appeal body to review detention orders constituted a breach of the ECHR, which had been part of the Austrian constitution since 1958. It took a condemnation from the ECHR for the Austrian government to appoint the Independent Administrative Senate to review detention orders in 1991 and

---

38 Asyl in Not, "Asylentscheidungen 1980–2015" (unpublished statistic data).
39 Hannes Tretter, *Temporary protection für bosnische Flüchtlinge in Europa: Länderberichte* (Wien: Verl. Österreich, 2000), 28–29.
40 Genner, "Asylverfahren," 436; §7 (1) Asylum Act 1991.

provide an opportunity for activist lawyers to challenge illegal practices.[41] A veritable battle over the lawful use of immigration detention was fought over a period of a few years between immigration police, the new review board, and lawyers; the latter managed to align detention practices with international law for some time.[42]

In addition to the decision-making practices of the immigration police, living conditions in Austrian detention facilities were another point of contention. In the 1990s, pre-removal detainees were kept in the same compounds as criminal prisoners and shared their terrible experiences. International control bodies such as the European Committee for the Prevention of Torture and Inhuman or Degrading Treatment or Punishment (CPT) and the United Nations Committee Against Torture (CAT) repeatedly raised concerns about the lack of information provided to foreign detainees, inadequate healthcare provisions, insufficient opportunities to contact counselors or lawyers, and high level of violence. After its first investigative visit to Austria, CPT concluded that detainees in Austrian prison facilities faced a "serious risk of . . . being illtreated while in police custody."[43] Toward the end of the 1990s, the violence was found to have become more racially selective and targeted more foreign male detainees than Austrian male detainees.[44] Due to these circumstances, CPT summarized the situation in Austrian detention facilities as unbearable, especially for minors.[45] It also found that occasional visits from international organizations were insufficient for guaranteeing respect of human rights standards in Austrian prisons and urged the government to establish an independent inspection body at the national level.[46] However, Löschnak did not respond to these claims during his time in office.

---

41 The detention of asylum seekers in an ongoing procedure was not in accordance with §7 (1) Asylum Act 1991 which accorded asylum seekers a preliminary authorization to stay.

42 Georg Bürstmayr, "Vom Urknall im österreichischen Fremdenrecht," in *Vom Umgang mit den "Anderen". Historische und menschenrechtliche Perspektiven der Abschiebung,* edited by Manfred Nowak and Edith Saurer (Wien: NWV – Neuer Wiss. Verl., 2013), 147, 154–55, 159–60 (Studienreihe des Ludwig-Boltzmann-Instituts für Menschenrechte 25).

43 Council of Europe, 3 October 1991, *Report to the Austrian Government on the visit to Austria carried out by the European Committee for the Prevention of Torture and Inhuman or Degrading Treatment or Punishment. from 20 May 1990 to 27 May 1990* (Strasbourg 1991), CPT/Inf (91) 10, 7.

44 Council of Europe, 21 June 2001, *Rapport au Gouvernement autrichien relatif à la visite en Autriche effectuée par le Comité européen pour la prévention de la torture et des peines ou traitements inhumains ou dégradants (CPT). du 19 au 30 septembre 1999* (Strasbourg 2001), CPT/Inf (2001), 11.

45 Margit Paier, "Zur Nicht-Akzeptanz einer Haft ohne Delikt. Öffentliche Kritik, Widerstand und Protest gegen die Schubhaft in Österreich," Diplomarbeit, Universität Wien, 2011, 120–21.

46 Council of Europe, "Report", 46.

When the interior minister had police investigate the social environment of the victims of a bombing attack against the Roma in the Austrian province of Burgenland, public calls to step down could no longer be warded off. As a result, Löschnak was replaced by fellow party member Caspar Einem, who was known for being more refugee-friendly.[47] One of his first initiatives was to abolish legislation adopted under his predecessor that caused the most hardship. In addition to a drafting a new asylum act, Einem also introduced improvements in detention pending deportation. He supported the establishment of an independent national inspection body for prisons, as recommended by CPT, but could not realize this project himself. The concept of the *lenient measure* (German: *gelinderes Mittel*)[48] was also introduced to encourage implementation officers to abstain from ordering detention if the ultimate goal of deportation could also be supported by ordering the individual to take residence at a specific location. Finally, Einem initiated negotiations to institutionalize a care system for people in deportation-related detention. However, his liberal approach attracted significant opposition; consequently, he resigned early.

The Asylum Act of 1997 prepared by Einem was adopted under his successor, Karl Schlögl. The care system for deportation-related detainees was institutionalized; however, the mandate to advise detainees on legal issues and help them with appeals against detention was not incorporated into contracts with non-governmental organizations (NGOs). In addition, Schlögl did not initially take any concrete steps to establish a prison inspection body, but the brutal suffocation and death of Nigerian detainee Marcus Omofuma on his deportation flight in 1999 forced him into action. In reaction to Omofuma's death, numerous demonstrations and months-long vigils were held, and attendees voiced criticisms against the Austrian pre-removal detention system and police and called for the minister's resignation. To calm the protesters, Schlögl conceded to CPT's repeated recommendations and established the Advisory Board on Human Rights (*Menschenrechtsbeirat*), which would operate as a national and independent control body to regularly investigate Austrian prison facilities. Throughout its existence, the board took a particular interest in the situation of asylum and migration-related detainees.[49]

---

47 Genner, "Asylverfahren," 435.

48 §66 Fremdengesetz 1997.

49 GEMMI – Gesellschaft für Menschenrechte von Marginalisierten und MigrantInnen, *1000 Jahre Haft. Operation Spring & institutioneller Rassismus Resümee einer antirassistischen Gruppe,* (Wien: Verein für antirassistische Öffentlichkeitsarbeit 2005), http://no -racism.net/upload/424899865.pdf (26 January 2022); Peter Slominski and Florian Trauner, "Die Europäisierung der Abschiebepolitik Österreichs. Mehr Handlungsoptionen für staatliche AkteurInnen oder mehr Schutz für Betroffene?," *Österreichische Zeitschrift für Politikwissenschaft* 43 (2014) 2: 163–164.

Despite growing criticism of the pre-removal detention system, the number of detentions remained high throughout the 1990s. This suggests that detention remained a high priority for immigration police. According to Table 1, detention increased by 40% (from 10,796 to 15,027 cases) between 1991 and 1999.[50] This corresponds to a 77% increase in the number of terminations of stay (German: *Aufenthaltsbeendigungen*) issued in the same time period. Deportation numbers did not follow the trend but remained constant at between 9,000 and 11,000 throughout the decade. This suggests that the increased use of detention did not improve the effectiveness of deportation.

Table 1: Terminations of stay, pre-removal detentions, and deportations in the 1990s

	Total number of terminations of stay (illegalized migrants and rejected asylum seekers)[a]	Total pre-removal detentions (illegalized migrants and rejected asylum seekers)	Total number of deportations (illegalized migrants and rejected asylum seekers)
1991	11,406	10,796	9,807
1992	11,521	11,908	7,356
1993	13,430	12,902	8,857
1994	14,478	14,675	9,951
1995	16,625	14,875	9,951
1996	20,147	14,718	10,996
1997	16,913	13,047	10,097
1998	15,974	13,815	9,544
1999	20,210	15,027	9,236

[a] These figures include removal decisions under the Aliens Police Act (German: *fremdenpolizeiliche Ausweisungsentscheidungen*) and prohibitions of stay (German: *Aufenthaltsverbote*). Source: Own compilation based on official data from the Ministry of the Interior, answers to parliamentary inquiries, national security reports, reports by the Court of Audit Austria, and other official sources.

However, the proportion of asylum seekers among the detained remains unknown because disaggregated statistics have only been available since 2005. However, an examination of asylum denials suggests that they declined in number between the beginning and the end of the decade (see Table 2).[51]

---

50 Bundesministerin für Inneres Maria Fekter, 23 January 2009, *Anfragebeantwortung betreffend "Schubhaftzahlen"*, 298/AB to 230/J (XXIV. GP) 2009, https://www.parlament.gv.at/PAKT/VHG/XXIV/AB/AB_00298/fnameorig_148206.html (27 January 2022).

51 As previously mentioned, a negative asylum decision does not immediately make a person detainable and deportable, as they may be protected from deportation under Articles 2, 3, or 8 of the European Convention of Human Rights.

Table 2: Negative asylum decisions between 1990 and 1999

	Number of negative asylum decisions
1990	11,784
1991	17,217
1992	21,196
1993	14,204
1994	8,335
1995	6,634
1996	8,032
1997	7,286
1998	3,491
1999	3,300

Source: Data provided by Ministry of Interior upon request.

At the beginning of the 1990s, pre-removal detention was systematically used against asylum seekers in Austria following a change in attitudes toward refugees. Namely, the image of refugees shifted from subjects in need of protection to economically motivated people who "merely" sought a better life. This translated to changes in policies and implementation practices, which became stricter. Political struggles and disputes pertaining to the detention of asylum seekers over this decade involved a limited circle of experts, activists, and politicians and focused on legal support for detainees and detention conditions. Toward the end of the 1990s, the system saw some minor improvements as part of the new Asylum Act of 1997 and in response to the brutal death of Marcus Omofuma in police custody.

2.   Early 2000s: Testing the Limits of Detainability and Creative Policy Making

Only weeks after the death of Omofuma, security forces launched the Second Republic's most extensive police operation, which targeted Black people for alleged drug criminality. More than 100 Africans were arrested in a drug raid and later charged with drug trafficking and membership in a criminal organization.[52] The investigative methods used by the police were criticized on many occasions, and the charges turned out to be unfounded in some cases.[53] However, at the time, media attention to police violence rapidly led to reporting on the figure of the "black drug dealer." The far-right Freedom Party stoked public sentiment in an

52 GEMMI, "1000 Jahre Haft," 12.
53 Walter Sauer, "Operation Spring," https://www.hdgoe.at/arbeitsmigration (17 February 2022).

overtly racist national election campaign in 1999 that linked asylum and international drug criminality.[54]

In the autumn of 1999, the Freedom Party came second in elections, while the prior government partiesslated lost a considerable number of voters. Following failed negotiations on the renewal of a coalition between the Social Democrats and the People's Party (who came first and third, respectively), the latter turned to the Freedom Party to form a coalition. Thus, the first center-right government was inaugurated in February 2000.

For the first time since 1970, the Ministry of the Interior went to the People's Party, which appointed Ernst Strasser. Contrary to expectations, significant political changes related to migration and asylum were not enacted in the first two years of the new government's reign. Strasser only focused on this agenda after new elections brought the same combination of parties into power but significantly strengthened the People's Party and weakened the Freedom Party. Thus, beginning in 2003, two of the initiatives that had already been listed on the government's agenda in 2000 became a priority: increasing the speed and efficiency of deportation and preventing resistance from pre-removal detainees.[55]

The discourse that accompanied these political undertakings revolved around the topic of asylum fraud. Asylum fraud is a political rather than legal term; it does not have a clear and unanimously understood meaning, but it usually refers to asylum seekers who manipulate the system to attain refugee status. In contrast to the economic refugee, which was used to justify restrictive migration and asylum policy making in the 1990s, the fraudulent asylum seeker was often linked with discourses on international crime. In addition to refugees themselves, their supporters (including social workers, legal counselors, and lawyers) were often reproached for harming the country. The political claims linked to this discourse called for reforms to an asylum system that was deemed too generous and a more efficient and effective deportation regime. The Freedom Party had pushed this agenda since the late 1990s, but the People's Party also promoted these ideas in their election campaign in 2002.[56]

As the discourse on asylum fraud became increasingly amplified, two groups of asylum seekers landed in the spotlight, as they were believed to be particularly deportable but extremely resistant: rejected asylum seekers who filed subsequent applications and asylum claimants covered by the Dublin Regulation. Beginning in 2003, the rights and legal safeguards of both groups were reduced, and they

---

54 Grösel, "Fremde von Staats wegen," 205; GEMMI, "1000 Jahre Haft," 25.

55 Österreichische Bundesregierung, *Österreich neu regieren. Regierungsprogramm 2000* (Wien: Bundeskanzleramt, 2000), 60.

56 Max Preglau, "Rechtsextrem oder postmodern? Über Rhetorik, Programmatik und Interaktionsformen der FPÖ und die Regierungspolitik der FPÖVP-Koalition," 2002, http://image s.derstandard.at/20021030/preglau.pdf (26 January 2022).

were targeted for rapid detention and deportation.[57] With regard to the first group, filing an asylum application after receiving a negative decision may be necessary due to changes in the political situation in the country of origin or new evidence. In the dominant narrative, however, subsequent applications served to evade deportation, since Austrian law protects asylum seekers from deportation as long as the asylum procedure is ongoing (German: *faktischer Abschiebeschutz*). Thus, subsequent applicants were often portrayed as prototypically fraudulent asylum seekers. Members of the other group were referred to as "Dublin cases" in reference to the Dublin Regulation,[58] a European agreement that specifies that the member state in which an asylum seeker first arrives on their journey to Europe is responsible for assessing the claim. The convention further regulates how asylum seekers apprehended outside the territory of the responsible country may be forcibly returned (or "transferred," in the language of the convention). Austria signed the convention in 1997, but it remained mostly irrelevant until the neighboring countries of Slovenia, Slovakia, the Czech Republic, and Hungary became EU members. Consequently, Austria was surrounded by Dublin signatory countries. Some believed that this development marked the end of new asylum applications in Austria,[59] although it was well-known that the convention was not as simple to implement as the northern countries of the EU had hoped. One article of the convention provides room for resistance and holds that, if a Dublin deportee is not deported within a specific timeframe, they have to be admitted to the asylum procedure in the country in which they are located. Given that reception and procedural standards considerably differ between Dublin countries and the likelihood of obtaining asylum is highly dependent on the country that assesses the claim, some asylum seekers go hiding until the deadline for their deportation has expired.

In 2003, Strasser proposed an amendment to the Asylum Act that considerably reduced rights and legal safeguards for these two groups and increased the use of force. Subsequent applicants were detainable the moment that they lodged another asylum claim and had to await the outcome of their case in jail. Dublin cases could be detained once the authorities found that another state was responsible, even if their opinion was challenged in court. The amendment was passed despite

---

57 §5a (1), §34 (1) Z3, §32 (2) Asylum Act 1997, version 2003.

58 The Dublin Convention came into force in 1997 in twelve countries. Austria implemented the convention later that year. Official Journal of the European Communities, "Convention determining the State responsible for examining applications for asylum lodged in one of the Member States of the European Communities," (97/C 254/01), https://eur-lex.europa.eu/legal-content/EN/TXT/PDF/?uri=CELEX:41997A0819(01)&from=EN (17 February 2022).

59 Barbara Rosenkranz, Helene Partik-Pablé, Elke Achleitner and Maximilian Hofmann, 9 July 2004, *Anfrage betreffend Umsetzung des Dublin-II-Abkommens. Anfrage an den Bundesminister für Inneres*, 2080/J (XXII. GP) 2004, https://www.parlament.gv.at/PAKT/VHG/XXII/J/J_02080/fname_024331.pdf (27 January 2022).

countless warnings from experts that such measures represented a breach of constitutional law.

As a result of the combined efforts of the two opposition parties Greens and Social Democrats, legal experts, and activists, the law was brought before the Constitutional Court and the questionable clauses were lifted. The minister was required to amend the law, which had nevertheless been in force for several months and legitimized the practice of detaining – and, in the case of Dublin cases, deporting – asylum claimants whose cases had not been conclusively decided.

Instead of simply amending the paragraphs that had been declared unconstitutional, Strasser devised a much more comprehensive legislative proposal that removed protection from deportation and detention for people suffering a post-traumatic stress disorder, extended the maximum duration of pre-removal detention, and permitted the force feeding of hunger strikers.[60] Opposition parties and activists mobilized enough outrage to stop the proposal from passing through parliament and force the minister to resign. His successor, Liese Prokop, was known for maintaining a more reconciliatory stance, and human rights activists hoped that she would re-establish communication with NGOs and asylum lawyers.

Prokop took office in December 2004. Meanwhile, two EU directives highlighted the need for significant reform of Austria's migration and asylum law. The minister treated this as an opportunity to develop an entirely new version of the Asylum and Aliens Police Act to replace the existing version.[61] Contrary to the hopes of refugee supporters, Prokop mostly collaborated with implementation officers during the policy formulation phase and sidelined NGO practitioners and asylum lawyers.[62] The resulting draft not only included the very paragraphs that prompted her predecessor's departure from office only months earlier but went even further. This was made possible by the People's Party electoral strength and the fact that its selection of a coalition partner after the next election was contingent on support for the revision, which led the Social Democrats abandon their understanding with the Greens to keep the government's migration and asylum politics in check. The Social Democrats' vote provided the center-right government with the legitimacy required for the legislative process, despite the reform's considerable development of coercive techniques. Hence, under the Asylum Act of 2005 and the Aliens Police Act of 2005 (which remain valid legal frameworks to this day), people diagnosed with post-traumatic stress disorder

---

60 Bernhard Perchinig, "Einwanderungs- und Integrationspolitik," in *Schwarz-Blau. Eine Bilanz des "Neu-Regierens"*, edited by Emmerich Tálos, (Wien–Münster: LIT-Verl., 2006), 299 (Politik und Zeitgeschichte 3).

61 Ibid., 298–301.

62 Genner, "Asylverfahren," 445.

were no longer exempt from Dublin deportations and thus from detention prior to removal,[63] the maximum length of deportation-related detention was raised from six to ten months,[64] and force feeding became an option for responding to hunger-striking detainees.[65] These measures were claimed to be necessary to end the overly generous asylum regime, remove fraudulent asylum seekers, and enforce rules and regulations.

Regarding the clauses that required amendment, policy makers found creative ways to increase the deportability of Dublin cases and subsequent applicants without violating constitutional principles. Under the Dublin procedure, instead of being detained after the first-instance rejection of their application (which had been ruled out by the Constitutional Court), asylum seekers were required to limit their physical mobility to the district in which their accommodation was located in the first twenty days after arrival. Detention remained an option, but the authorities had to provide written notification to the asylum seeker that they had found clear indications of another country being responsible for the assessment of their claim and that deportation was anticipated. From the perspective of policy makers, the asylum procedure became a de facto removal procedure after this notification, which made detention legitimate. In terms of deportability, the new policies proved efficient. The restriction on mobility not only made asylum seekers more vulnerable to detention by police but also inhibited contact between asylum seekers and independent lawyers, activists, or peers, thereby preventing their access to crucial information about rights and options.[66]

Concerning subsequent applicants, policy makers removed the suspensive effect (German: *aufschiebende Wirkung*) of appeals, thereby making first-instance decisions immediately enforceable. The suspensive effect is a matter of legal safeguard in administrative law, which guarantees that a decision will not be executed if an appeal is pending. In cases involving subsequent asylum applicants, withdrawing this safeguard was presented as legitimate because a previous case had already been rejected. In effect, this once again made detention and deportation lawful practices in ongoing cases.[67]

---

63 This was done by revoking §24b (1) Asylum Act 1997, version 2003.
64 §80 (4) Aliens' Police Act 2005.
65 §78 (6) Aliens' Police Act 2005.
66 The combination of these policies had severe consequences for some asylum seekers. Chechens, who usually entered Europe through Poland, faced the real risk of chain deportation: first from Austria to Poland, then from Poland to Chechnya. Before the new laws entered into force, independent lawyers warned clients about the possible consequences of a deportation to Poland. The new provisions disabled contact to these lawyers and made resistance to Dublin deportations extremely difficult. Genner, "Asylverfahren," 442–44.
67 Frühwirth and Rössl, "Österreichs Asylpolitik".

Despite the back and forth of legislative activities during this period, pre-removal detention was ultimately expanded to a broader target group, including asylum claimants whose claims were still being assessed (e.g., Dublin cases, asylum seekers who filed subsequent applications, and criminal prisoners who sought asylum).[68] Furthermore, the instrument's effectiveness was increased by lengthening maximum detention terms and raising the lawful use of force in cases of resistance (e.g., against hunger strikers). Lastly, with the territorial movement restriction for asylum claimants under the Dublin procedure, the first non-detention type of movement restriction was developed and opened the door to similar measures in the future.

3.   2005 to 2016 Toward a Governmental Mode in the Use of Movement Restrictions

In the years following the center-right government, more scandals pertaining to immigration detention emerged in Austria. Once again, the victims tended to be young African men. In October 2005, 18-year-old Gambian Yankuba Ceesay died in detention after a seven-day hunger strike. Although he had lost a considerable amount of weight over a short period, neither the medical staff, social workers, nor guards felt compelled to act. A second incident occurred only months later. In April 2006, a Gambian detainee named Bakary Jassey, who was married to an Austrian and the father of two children, successfully resisted his deportation. Subsequently, the supervising police officers brutally tortured and threatened to kill him. Independent investigations into both cases confirmed the prevailing culture of violence and impunity in Austria's pre-removal detention system.[69]

In 2007, the European Commission evaluated the first phase of the Common European Asylum System, expressed concerns about the excessive use of immigration detention in some member states, and reiterated that detention should be a measure of last resort. The year after, immigration detention became the focus of EU regulation as part of the Return Directive (2008/115/EC), which combined liberal and restrictive approaches. On the one hand, the directive set strict limits on the lawful application of detention by reiterating the international

---

68 Roland Frühwirth and Ines Rössl, "Teil II: Österreichs Asylpolitik. Ständiger Entzug des Zugangs zum Recht" 18 January, 2016, https://mosaik-blog.at/teil-ii-oesterreichs-asylpolitik-staendiger-entzug-des-zugangs-zum-recht/ (27 January 2022).

69 United Nations Committee against Torture, 27 January 2016, *Concluding observations on the sixth periodic report of Austria,* CAT/C/AUT/CO/6 2016, 7; Menschenrechtsbeirat, *Gesundheitsversorgung in Schubhaft. Bericht und Empfehlungen des Menschenrechtsbeirates anlässlich des Todes von Yankuba Ceesay im PAZ Linz* (Wien: Geschäftsstelle des Menschenrechtsbeirates, Bundesministerium für Inneres, 2007), 7–9, 24, 37.

law principle that administrative detention had to serve the purpose of securing a removal procedure or a deportation process and could only be upheld for "as long as removal arrangements are in progress and executed with due diligence."[70] In addition, lenient measures should be prioritized and detention should be reserved for cases in which goals cannot be reached through less intrusive alternatives, "in particular when: (a) there is a risk of absconding or (b) the third-country national concerned avoids or hampers the preparation of return or the removal process."[71] On the other hand, the directive encoded the lawful application of detention against families and minors at the European level. Detaining children was not legal in all EU member states and was highly contested in countries in which it was practiced.[72]

In addition to heightened scrutiny by international organizations, public interest in deportation grew during this period. Shortly after Günther Platter assumed leadership of the Ministry of Internal Affairs, he prompted asylum authorities to close asylum cases that had already been pending for many years and enforce negative decisions. Consequently, within a short time period, 8,000 individuals and 2,000 to 3,000 families were at risk of deportation.[73] Many lived in the countryside, had jobs, and were considered well-integrated into society. From the beginning, attempts to enforce these removal decisions were met with resistance by asylum claimants as well as their neighbors and friends in local communities. Moreover, high-ranking politicians and members of the public demanded changes to Austria's migration policy and the right to remain in the country for well-integrated individuals and families. In September 2007, a schoolgirl named Arigona Zogaj went into hiding to escape her family's deportation to Kosovo and threatened political representatives with suicide. As a result, the first major anti-deportation campaign emerged in Austria.

The right wing of the political spectrum also became more involved with the topic of deportation. After the Freedom Party once again became the opposition party in 2005, it politicized the inefficiency of deportation, a cause that it had espoused in the late 1990s but largely set aside while serving as junior partner in

---

70 Article 15 and 17, "Directive 2008/115/EC of the European Parliament and of the Council of 16 December 2008 on common standards and procedures in Member States for returning illegally staying third-country nationals".

71 Ibid.

72 Ibid.

73 Max Preglau, "Umbruch der politischen Kultur in Österreich: von der schwarz-blau/orange Wende 2000 über das rot-schwarze Interregnum 2006–2017 und Schwarz/ Türkis-Blau 2.0 zu Türkis-Grün. Max Preglaus Regierungs-Watch," 27 May 2022, https://www.uibk.ac.at/soziol ogie/team/max-preglau/regierungsbeobachtung/info_fpoe_preglau_max.pdf (2 June 2022), 274–275.

the coalition with the People's Party.[74] Particularly during the following legislative period (Faymann I, 2008 to 2013), members of parliament (MPs) from the Freedom Party used parliamentary questions in an almost systematic manner to enquire about the discrepancy between the number of rejected asylum cases and the number of rejected asylum seekers who were actually deported from Austria. They identified a lack of return agreements with countries of origin, resistance practices used by detainees, and civil society protests as primary causes for the suspension of deportation in many cases, which rendered the instrument ineffective.[75] Indeed, between 2005 and 2013, the discrepancy between the number of expulsion orders issued against rejected asylum seekers and actual deportations was considerable. According to Table 3, only between 2% to 10% of rejected asylum seekers were deported after a removal decision. However, it is important to note that rejected asylum seekers become eligible for deportation only after the timeframe for individual departure provided in the removal decision has elapsed. Since individual departures are not registered by the Austrian state, it is impossible to know how many of these asylum seekers leave the country on their own. Moreover, during this period, the emphasis was on returning deportable non-citizens through assisted "voluntary" return programs.[76] Between 2004 and 2013, assisted "voluntary" returns increased from roughly over 1,000 to over 3,500, peaking at over 4,000 in 2009 and 2010 (see Table 6).[77] In addition to rejected asylum seekers, these numbers include other non-citizens whose legal stay was terminated during this period.

However, evidence shows that the "deportation gap"[78] is a relevant phenomenon in many European countries, especially with regard to rejected asylum

---

74 See for example parliamentary inquiry 6658/J, XX. GP, FPÖ, 16.07.1999, "der Abgeordneten Helene Partik-Pablé an den Bundesminister für Inneres betreffend in Österreich lebende illegale Fremde".

75 Sieglinde Rosenberger and Judith Welz, "Das Abschieberegime fast außer Kontrolle? Parlamentarische Anfragen zwischen Menschenrechten und Souveränität," in *Migration und Integration – wissenschaftliche Perspektiven aus Österreich, Jahrbuch 4/2018*, edited by Jennifer Schellenbacher Carvill et al. (Göttingen: V&R unipress, Vienna Univ. Press, 2018), 62–66 (Migrations- und Integrationsforschung Band 010). Parliamentary inquiry 890/J XXIV. GP, FPÖ, 13.02.2009, "des Abgeordneten Dr. Walter Rosenkranz und weiterer Abgeordneter an die Bundesministerin für Inneres betreffend kriminelle Ausländer, die sich mit Asylanträgen ihren Aufenthalt ertrotzen"; parliamentary inquiry 5296/J XXIV. GP, FPÖ, 07.05.2010, "des Abgeordneten Herbert und weiterer Abgeordneter an die Bundesministerin für Inneres betreffend Ausweisung und Abschiebung".

76 The voluntary nature of these programs is doubtful, especially in cases in which individuals were left with a choice between forced removal or assisted return.

77 In Austria, rejected asylum seekers and illegalized migrants could opt for a "voluntary" return if they were in detention. Thus, some individuals may be included in statistics on detention and "voluntary" returns.

78 Matthew J Gibney, "Asylum and the Expansion of Deportation in the United Kingdom," *Government and Opposition* 43 (2008) 2: 149.

seekers. The reasons are manifold. On a practical level, deportations are sometimes not enforceable due to a lack of travel documents or because no transportation mode is available. On a legal level, deportations occasionally have to be postponed or cancelled because they constitute a breach of constitutional or human rights provisions, such as when a deportable person is in a critical health situation or has established strong social ties in the host community.[79]

Table 3: Removal decisions against rejected asylum seekers and deportations of rejected asylum seekers between 2005 and 2013

	Removal decisions against rejected asylum seekers	Deportations of rejected asylum seekers
2005	4,552	462
2006	3,782	349
2007	6,646	455
2008	7,968	330
2009	13,531	477
2010	13,290	579
2011	11,553	445
2012	10,436	292
2013	10,379	194

Source: Own compilation based on official data from the Ministry of Interior, answers to parliamentary inquiries, national security reports, reports by the Court of Audit Austria, and other official sources.

Since pre-removal detention must stop and a detainee must be released when it becomes obvious that a deportation cannot be implemented, obstacles to deportation may also represent obstacles to detention. As stated in empirical Section 1, the numbers of deportations and detentions were similarly high in the 1990s. Between 2000 and 2013, the number of annual deportations significantly decreased compared to the number of detentions. This suggests that detention led to deportation in much fewer cases than in the previous decade. However, this conclusion must be carefully drawn since an individual may be detained several times but deported only once. More reliable information was provided in a report by the Austrian Court of Audit. According to the report, pre-removal detention did not result in the (forced or voluntary) departure of the detainee in 62% of cases from 2010 to 2015. In 36% of cases, detainees had to be released due to the abovementioned legal or practical obstacles or physical resistance from the de-

---

79 Ilker Ataç, "Deserving Shelter: Conditional Access to Accommodation for Rejected Asylum Seekers in Austria, the Netherlands, and Sweden," *Journal of immigrant & refugee studies* 17 (2019) 1: 49.

tainee, especially in the form of hunger strikes.[80] Thus, toward the end of the 2000s, deportation and detention (along with human rights concerns) became the subjects of discussions about effectiveness.

The developments outlined above created a complicated situation for policy makers, with more critical scrutiny on the one hand and increased pressure to increase the effectiveness of detention and deportation on the other. Subsequent governments addressed this dilemma by gradually marginalizing detention as priority measure for facilitating deportation while compensating for the loss of control with an alternative system based on restrictions and obligations for rejected asylum seekers and asylum seekers pending decision. Under the new system, detention still lurked in the background as a measure to turn to when restrictions and obligations were not respected.

Minister of the Interior Günther Platter of the People's Party, who took office after the relaunch of the so-called "grand coalition" between the Social Democrats and the People's Party in 2007, made greater use of *lenient measures* as alternatives to pre-removal detention, which foreshadowed the transformation process. The option had been available since 1997/8 but saw little use during the coalition with the Freedom Party, except for the first and last year of government. Between 2007 and 2016, the average share of lenient measures rose to 17.6%,[81] compared to 6.4% between 2000 and 2006 (see Table 4).

Table 4: Use of lenient measures between 2000 and 2020

	∑ Pre-removal detention and lenient measures	*Of which lenient measures*
2000	16,263	1,934 (11.9%)
2001	17,987	681 (3.8%)
2002	12,623	807 (6.4%)
2003	11,767	618 (5.2%)
2004	9,404	363 (3.9%)
2005	7,748	285 (3.7%)
2006	9,621	927 (9.6%)
2007	8,118	1,158 (14.3%)
2008	7,107	1,809 (25.1%)
2009	–	615 (until April 2009)
2010	7,557	1,404 (18.6%)
2011	6,167	1,012 (16.4%)

80 Rechnungshof Österreich, *Vollzug der Schubhaft mit Schwerpunkt Anhaltezentrum Vordernberg; Follow-up-Überprüfung: Bericht des Rechnungshofes*, (Wien 2019), Reihe BUND 25, 22, https://www.rechnungshof.gv.at/rh/home/home/home_7/Anhaltezentrum_Vordernberg.pdf.
81 For 2009, the available data is incomplete.

Table 4 *(Continued)*

	∑ Pre-removal detention and lenient measures	*Of which lenient measures*
2012	5,486	925 (16.9%)
2013	4,942	771 (15.6%)
2014	–	–
2015	2,453	571 (23.3%)
2016	1,739	178 (10.2%)
2017	5,160	345 (6.7%)
2018	4,167	299 (7.2%)
2019	4,507	402 (8.9%)
2020	3,578	653 (18.3%)

Source: Own compilation based on official data from the Ministry of Interior, answers to parliamentary inquiries, national security reports, reports by the Court of Audit Austria, and other official sources.

Platter's successor and fellow party member, Maria Fekter, backed another initiative that aimed to improve assessments of the Austrian detention system. Fekter initiated negotiations with communities to construct the first standalone immigration detention facility in response to numerous recommendations from national and international human rights organizations. The "competence center,"[82] as the government called the detention facility, was intended as a best practice model for Europe in terms of architectural design, managerial standards, and service provision. However, the involvement of private companies at all stages, from the planning of the building to day-to-day operations, considerably impeded the process. As a result, the facility had still not been constructed by the time the next scandal emerged in Austria. Conversely, the new scandal accelerated the construction of standalone detention centers (German: *Schubhaftzentren*), starting with a very particular type of facility: family detention centers. In the autumn of 2010, armed police officers fetched a father and his twin daughters who were to be detained prior to removal from a private shelter in which "especially well-integrated and blameless" (author's translation) families threatened with deportation were housed by activists.[83] Supporters filmed the operation and widely disseminated the footage. The images, which showed armed police officers taking minors into custody, antagonized large segments of society. Over the following months, a strong civil society movement called

---

82 Österreichische Bundesregierung, "Regierungsprogramm 2008–2013. Gemeinsam für Österreich – Regierungsprogramm für die XXIV. Gesetzgebungsperiode" (Wien: Bundeskanzleramt, 2008), 106. Österreichische Bundesregierung, "Österreich neu regieren. Regierungsprogram 2000" (Wien: Bundeskanzleramt, 2000), 60.

83 Verein Purple Sheep, "Das Freunde Schützen Haus," http://www.purplesheep.at/index.php?i=psDasHaus (18 March 2021).

Against Injustice, which was backed by varous media outlets, was established. It aimed to end the detention of children and make children's rights part of the Austrian constitution. Fekter came under intense pressure but refused to prohibit the detention of children. Instead, she announced the establishment of a family detention center where families could stay together and guards would be unarmed and out of uniform.[84] The facility opened within weeks, predating the inauguration of the "competence center" by three years. More detention facilities were built by successor Johanna Mikl-Leitner (People's Party), who announced in 2015 that there was sufficient capacity to conduct immigration detention entirely at the new facilities.[85] Reactions to the detention centers were far from unanimous. While some authorities portrayed them as alternatives to detention,[86] critics suspected that their goal was to obscure the coerciveness and violence that characterized any form of arrest. For the Austrian government, the step proved to be a success because national and international reports on Austria's detention system were no longer catastrophic. For instance, the national ombudsman, a regular critic of the detention system, called it "rather good" following a visit to the largest facility in Vordernberg (province of Steiermark) in 2016.[87] However, it must be mentioned that almost no detainees were present on the day of the visit since the attempt to reduce detention numbers had taken shape.[88]

The number of detentions has consistently declined since 2002. However, the pool of non-citizens who were issued a decision to terminate their stay in Austria remained between 44% and 77% between 2000 and 2007. In 2008, this rate declined to 38% and stabilized at approximately 30% until 2016, except in 2014 (see Table 5). In absolute terms, a 50% decrease in the number of detentions occurred between 2014 and 2015. The number of detentions decreased again in 2016 before rising the following year (see Table 5).[89]

---

84 Sonja Jell, "Alternative zur Schubhaft," in *Öffentliche Sicherheit – Das Magazin des Innenministeriums* (2012) 5–6: 25–26, https://bmi.gv.at/magazinfiles/2012/05_06/files/zinnergasse.pdf (27 January 2022).

85 Volksanwaltschaft, *Sonderbericht Anhaltezentrum Vordernberg*, (Wien: Volksanwaltschaft, 2015), https://volksanwaltschaft.gv.at/downloads/1i6dp/SB_Vordernberg.pdf (26 January 2022), 136.

86 mac, "Zehn Prozent mehr Abschiebungen in Wien. Fremdenpolizei 'zufrieden' mit umstrittenem Familien-Schubhaftzentrum," *Der Standard*, 27 January, 2017, https://www.derstandard.at/story/1295570932006/anstieg-zehn-prozent-mehr-abschiebungen-in-wien (26 January 2022).

87 Volksanwaltschaft, 'Sonderbericht,' 50.

88 Ibid.

89 For a discussion of statistical data for the years between 2016 and 2020, see empirical Section 4.

Table 5: Terminations of stay, pre-removal detentions, and deportations between 2000 and 2020

	Total number of terminations of stay (illegalized migrants and rejected asylum seekers)[a]	Pre-removal detention total and relative to terminations of stay	Total number of deportations (illegalized migrants and rejected asylum seekers)
2000	21,495	14,329 (66.7%)	9,638
2001	22,591	17,306 (76.6%)	8,324
2002	23,705	11,816 (49.9%)	6,842
2003	22,588	11,149 (49.4%)	8,037
2004	20,646	9,041 (43.8%)	5,274
2005	16,491	7,463 (45.3%)	4,277
2006	12,813	8,694 (67.9%)	4,090
2007	13,461	6,960 (51.7%)	2,838
2008	14,162	5,398 (38.2%)	2,026
2009	20,219	5,996 (29.7%)	2,481
2010	20,165	6,153 (30.5%)	2,577
2011	16,285	5,155 (31.7%)	1,968
2012	14,439	4,561 (28%)	1,852
2013	14,604	4,171 (28.6%)	1,903
2014	7,266	3,943 (54.3%)	1,619
2015	6,668	1,882 (28.2%)	1,900
2016	6,030	1,561 (25.9%)	2,289
2017	7,032	4,815 (68.5%)	3,162
2018	–	3,868	4,661
2019	28,148	4,105 (14.6%)	5,357
2020	39,293	2,925 (7.4%)	3,569

[a] Figures include removal decisions under the Aliens Police Act (German: *fremdenpolizeiliche Ausweisungsentscheidungen*), prohibitions of stay (German: *Aufenthaltsverbote*), removal decisions under the Asylum Act (German: *asylrechtliche Ausweisungsentscheidungen*), and return decisions (German: *Rückkehrentscheidungen*). Removal decisions against rejected asylum seekers were renamed return decisions following EU legislation in 2014. Source: Own compilation based on official data from the Ministry of Interior, answers to parliamentary inquiries, national security reports, reports by the Court of Audit Austria, the Bundesamt für Fremdenwesen und Asyl, and other official sources. – No data available.

The decline in number of detentions may be partly explained by an increase in the use of lenient measures since 2006, a greater emphasis on assisted "voluntary" return programs since 2000,[90] and changes in policy and the practice of pre-removal detention after 2007.

---

90 National Contact Point Austria within the European Migration Network (EMN), Interna-

As previously mentioned, the use of lenient measures as an alternative to detention rose from 6.44% between 2000 and 2006 to 17.6%[91] between 2007 and 2016 (see Table 4). Moreover, the prioritization of "voluntary" return programs since 2000 has contributed to a decrease in detentions. Accurate data is available after 2004. Table 5 shows that assisted returns as a part of state-sponsored return programs exceeded 1,000 in 2004, 2,000 in 2006, and 4,000 in 2009 and stabilized at around 3,000 between 2011 and 2013.[92]

Table 6: Assisted "voluntary" returns between 2004 and 2013

	Total number of assisted "voluntary" returns (illegalized migrants and rejected asylum seekers)
2004	1,158
2005	1,406
2006	2,189
2007	2,164
2008	2,736
2009	4,088
2010	4,517
2011	3,400
2012	3,211
2013	3,512

Source: Own compilation based on official data from the Ministry of Interior, answers to parliamentary inquiries, national security reports, reports by the Court of Audit Austria, and other official sources.

Another reason for the decrease in detentions was changes in practice. For example, the significant 50% decline in the number of detentions in 2015 is most likely attributable to the increased use of apprehension orders (German: *Festnahmeauftrag*). Established by the Asylum Act of 1991, this instrument had rarely been applied before 2015. Then, apprehension orders became the preferred form of detention in cases in which no obstacles or resistance were expected. Apprehension orders permitted the detention of rejected asylum seekers for a period of no longer than 72 hours. Their use required the fulfillment of the same pre-conditions as pre-removal detention. However, appeals were not permis-

---

tional Organization for Migration, "Rückkehrmigration in Österreich: Österreichischer Beitrag zum Europäischen Forschungsprojekt III: 'Return Migration in the EU Member States'," https://www.emn.at/wp-content/uploads/2017/01/Return_Migration_AT.pdf (10 February 2022).

91 For 2009, the available data is incomplete.

92 Since rejected asylum seekers and illegalized migrants in Austria may opt for a "voluntary" return from detention, some individuals may be represented in statistics on detention and "voluntary" returns.

sible.[93] Since arrests following apprehension orders do not formally constitute pre-removal detention, they do not appear in statistics.

Finally, the reduction in the number of detentions also evidenced a paradigm shift in detention policy spurred by Minister of the Interior Maria Fekter. As part of the shift, detention was gradually replaced by obligations to cooperate and non-detention movement restrictions as the primary control instrument for deportees from 2009 onward. Over time, the system of obligations and restrictions was extended to target groups other than deportable subjects. As a rule, detention remained linked to these obligations and restrictions, as any violation constituted a reason for detention (German: *Schubhafttatbestand*).[94] Thus, the nature of detention was altered, and it was used to more selectively target individuals who could not be disciplined by the other control system.

Politically, the paradigm shift was a success. The number of detentions continued to decline, and the repressive nature of the alternative system did not become a significant point of public contention. The course was held by Fekter's successors and fellow party members Johanna Mikl-Leitner (in office April 2011 to April 2016) and Wolfgang Sobotka (April 2016 to December 2017) and modestly pushed forward by Herbert Kickl from the Freedom Party (December 2017 to May 2019).

To illustrate the paradigm shift, the following paragraphs contain some examples. As mentioned above, the deportation of Dublin cases had been a matter of high priority since the early 2000s. However, detention to facilitate deportation was only applicable in certain situations, as confirmed in a ruling by the Constitutional Court. In reaction to the ruling, policy makers in 2005 employed a combination of territorial movement restrictions at the beginning of the Dublin procedure and detention once deportation under the Dublin Regulation became probable. Four years later, detention was replaced by a reporting requirement to police responding to the paradigm shift.[95] The reporting requirement, which effectively constituted a mobility restriction due to the frequency of compulsory reporting, remained tied to detention, as any breach constituted a reason for pre-removal arrest (assuming that the general conditions for immigration detention were fulfilled). Movement restrictions for Dublin cases were expanded in 2011[96] and 2018,[97] remaining linked to detention each time.

---

93 Herbert Langthaler, "Freiheitsentzug Als Abschreckung," *Asyl Aktuell* (2020) 3: 28.

94 In response to the European Commission's Return Directive requirement that detention should be used only if an individual is at risk of absconding or hampering the deportation process, Austrian policy makers redefined all legal reasons for detention as proof of the risk of absconding, including breaches of movement restrictions and obligations to cooperate.

95 §15a (1) Asylum Act 2005, version 2010.

96 §15 (3a) Asylum Act 2005, version 2011.

97 §28 (2) Asylum Act 2005, version 2018.

Moreover, as part of the paradigm shift, rejected asylum seekers were obligated from 2009 onward to collaborate with authorities to prepare and implement their own deportation, especially with regard to arranging a valid travel document.[98] Again, a refusal constituted a legal reason for detention.[99] This attempt to compel the collaboration of rejected asylum seekers in their own deportation failed to produce the expected results, as international law does not allow pre-removal detention to be upheld when deportation is unlikely to occur any time soon. Hence, rejected asylum seekers who did not possess valid travel documents were not deportable even if this was due to their refusal to collaborate with authorities and thus could not be kept in detention for an extended period. By 2015, policy makers had found a solution to this issue. If detention was not possible within the framework of migration and asylum law, non-compliant rejected asylum seekers would be arrested based on administrative law. Thus, detention to compel compliance (GE: *Beugehaft*) was made available for un-cooperative rejected asylum seekers: a prison sentence of up to six weeks, which could be indefinitely repeated.[100] That way, non-compliant rejected asylum seekers could be imprisoned without violating international and constitutional law.[101]

In 2017, another way to increase pressure on non-compliant rejected asylum seekers was introduced. Policy-makers adopted a clause that allowed authorities to order rejected asylum seekers to live in a specific location and limit their mobility to its vicinity.[102] This laid the groundwork for changes to come. When another version of the center right coalition government came to power in December 2017 and Herbert Kickl of the Freedom Party assumed leadership of the Ministry of the Interior from the People's Party after seventeen years, he turned the most unpopular and remote accommodation centers into so-called return centers to host non-compliant rejected asylum seekers. Moreover, they were forbidden to stray too far from the facilities under threat of immigration detention. Given that immigration detention would not be applicable in most cases due to the lack of travel documents or other practical obstacles, precautions were

---

98 It is important to note that, while obligations to cooperate also exist in other areas of administrative law, they do not compel individuals to cooperate against their personal interests. Reinhard Klaushofer, "Probleme bei der Ermittlung des Sachverhalts," in *Das Asylrecht als Experimentierfeld: Eine Analyse seiner Besonderheiten aus vergleichender Sicht*, edited by Franz Merli and Magdalena Pöschl, (Wien: Manz, 2017), 147–74.

99 §76 (2a) 4. Aliens' Police Act 2005, version 2009.

100 §46 (2a) Aliens' Police Act 2005, version 2015.

101 After minor objections by the High Court, a slightly modified version of the law was passed in 2017. The first attempt was blocked by the Constitutional Court for its vague definition of compliance. In 2017, compliance was defined as cooperation in the organization of travel documents.

102 §§52a and 57 Aliens' Police Act 2005, version 2017.

taken this time. Thus, residents at the return centers could be fined up to 5.000 EURO for moving beyond the district boundaries in which their accommodation was located.[103] If rule breakers were unable to pay the fine, they could be taken into custody (German: *Ersatzfreiheitsstrafe*). Like compensatory custody, detention to compel compliance replaced immigration detention when it was not legally available.

Finally, after movement restrictions were tested with rejected asylum seekers, they were expanded to asylum seekers in ongoing cases in 2017. Therefore, movement restrictions were decoupled from the primary purpose of facilitating deportation. Authorities began to sanction various types of undesired behavior through residence orders (German: *Anordnung zur Unterkunftnahme*), including breaches of accommodation centers' house rules, alleged criminal activity, or non-cooperation with asylum case workers.[104] Following the new logic, asylum seekers under residence orders were forbidden from moving beyond the boundaries of the district in which they lived. If they did, they realized a reason for detention, which could become relevant once the asylum claim was decided in the negative.[105]

After 2005, an increase in critical scrutiny of the detention system and growing political pressure to raise the effectiveness of detention and deportation led Austrian decision makers to initiate reforms. Starting in 2007, lenient measures were used more frequently as alternatives to detention and first attempts to establish standalone immigration detention facilities were undertaken. However, the new compounds did not reach their full capacity since imprisonment was reserved for a relatively small number of individuals who were deemed "problematic"[106] following a paradigm shift in 2009. This led to a paradoxical effect:

---

103 §121 (1a) Aliens' Police Act 2005, version 2017.

104 §15b Asylum Act version 2017.

105 Such an approach was in accordance with EU law and less severe than the punitive measures allowed in the European legal text. In 2003, the Reception Conditions Directive allowed the restriction of asylum seekers' free movement if this was deemed necessary to ensure public order or the smooth progression of the asylum procedure (SISI: Which procedure?) (Art 7 (2 +3) Reception Conditions Directive). The recast of the Reception Conditions Directive in 2013 went significantly further by permitting the detention of asylum seekers who were still awaiting a decision for a variety of reasons, including to determine their identity, their right to enter the country, or, if deemed necessary, reasons of "national security or public order" (Art 8 (3f) Reception Conditions Directive (recast)). Meanwhile, asylum seekers in an ongoing procedure are detainable: Langthaler, "Freiheitsentzug," 32.

106 National Contact Point Austria within the European Migration Network, *Illegal Immigration in Austria. A survey of recent Austrian migration research, Austrian contribution to the European Research Study Project II: "Illegally Resident Third Country Nationals in the EU Member States: State Approaches Towards Them and Their Profile and Social Situation"* (Wien: International Organization for Migration, 2005, 48, https://www.emn.at/wp-content/uploads/2017/01/Illegal-Immigration_FINAL_VERSION_ENG.pdf (26 January 2022)).

conflicts and violent incidents increased as numbers of detainees decreased and conditions in detention facilities improved.[107]

Thus, the marginalization of detention did not mean that the state relinquished control over deportable subjects. Instead, it diversified and stratified its techniques. While a growing number of rejected asylum seekers were subject to a system of obligations and restrictions, a decreasing number of individuals faced detention, namely those who disrespected or violated these obligations.

4.   After the "Long Summer of Migration":[108] The Renaissance of Detention

Four years into the war in Syria and with a worsening security situation in Afghanistan, the arrival of refugees via the Mediterranean Sea had been on the rise since 2014. Starting from the spring of 2015, large numbers of refugees passed from Turkey into Greece and followed the Balkan route to the north.[109]

Responding to the tragic deaths of 72 refugees who had suffocated in the back of a cooling truck on an Austrian highway and the march of hundreds of refugees from Hungary toward the Austrian border, the Austrian and the German governments declared their borders open to refugees on September 5, 2015. In the following weeks and months, the Ministry of the Interior accommodated approximately 10,000 new arrivals per month with support from municipalities, NGOs, churches, and individual volunteers. Between 2014 and 2015, asylum applications in Austria more than doubled, increasing from 28,000 to 88,300.[110]

In the years following what is known today among migration scholars as "the long summer of migration," the return of illegalized non-citizens became a priority in the EU and its member states. In 2017, the European Commission provided recommendations on how to implement the Return Directive of

---

107 Own calculation based on parliamentary inquiries. Bundesminister für Inneres Karl Schlögl, 19 May 1999, *Anfragebeantwortung betreffend "Selbstmorde, Selbstmordversuche und -beschädigungen in Schubhaft"*, 5586/AB to 5940/J (XX. GP) 1999, https://www.parlament.gv.a t/PAKT/VHG/XX/AB/AB_05586/fname_135473.pdf (28 January 2022); Bundesminister für Inneres Herbert Kickl, 15 November 2018, *Anfragebeantwortung betreffend "Zustände und Bedingungen in österreichischen (Polizei-)Anhaltezentren"*, 1681/AB to 1692/J (XXVI.GP) 2018, https://www.parlament.gv.at/PAKT/VHG/XXVI/AB/AB_01681/imfname_721304.pdf (27 January 2022).

108 Bernd Kasparek and Mark Speer, "Of hope: Ungarn und der lange Sommer der Migration," https://bordermonitoring.eu/ungarn/2015/09/of-hope/ (11 February 2022).

109 Sabine Hess et al., "Der lange Sommer der Migration. Krise, Rekonstitution und ungewisse Zukunft des europäischen Grenzregimes," in *Der lange Sommer der Migration*, edited by Sabine Hess et al. (Berlin–Hamburg: Assoziation A, 2017), 6–24, here 10–11.

110 Bundesministetrium für Inneres, "Asylstatistik 2015," 3, https://www.bmi.gv.at/301/Stati stiken/files/Jahresstatistiken/Asyl_Jahresstatistik_2015.pdf (2 June 2022).

2008.[111] Besides increasing the effectiveness of return policy, an increase in deportations was also intended to function as a deterrent to future migration and flight movements.[112]

Accordingly, the core objective of the Aliens Law Amendment Act adopted in October 2017 by the Austrian National Assembly[113] was to "step up the enforcement of returns of rejected asylum seekers." Thus, detention once again came into focus. As part of the amendment, the maximum duration of pre-removal detention was raised to eighteen months to ensure that difficult-to-implement deportations could be executed.[114]

At the level of implementation, the use of lenient measures decreased once more. According to the UN High Commissioner on Human Rights, bureaucrats used their discretionary power to identify the risk of absconding in an increasing number of cases.[115] Consequently, the use of alternatives to detention decreased to 7.6% (see Table 4). As shown in Table 5, the number of detentions tripled in 2017 (4,815 cases) compared to a historical low of 1,739 cases in 2016 before stabilizing at approximately 3,000 to 4,100 cases until 2020. Compared to non-citizens who were issued a termination of stay, the proportion of detainees rose to 68% in 2017 but decreased to 14.6% in 2019 and to 7.4% in 2020. Within these two years, the Bundesamt for Fremdenwesen and Asyl (the primary office for matters of asylum and migration since 2014) managed to address the backlog of open cases, which explains why the number of terminations of stay considerably increased.

It is important to note that the effectiveness of detention finally increased. Between 2016 and 2018, the percentage of detainees whose detention ended in a forced or assisted departure rose to 83%, compared to 62% between 2010 and 2015.[116] According to the Court of Audit, this was attributable to the manner in which pre-removal detainees are counselled in Austria.[117] Under the first center-

---

111 European Commission, "Recommendation of 7.3.2017 on making returns more effective when implementing the Directive 2008/115/EC of the European Parliament and of the Council" (European Commission, Brussels, 2017), https://ec.europa.eu/home-affairs/sys tem/files/2020-09/20170302_commission_recommendation_on_making_returns_more_ef fective_en.pdf (11 February 2022).

112 Office of the United Nations High Commissioner for Human Rights (OHCHR), "Report of mission to Austria focusing on the human rights of migrants, particularly in the context of return: 15.–18. October 2018" (United Nations 2018), 4, https://www.ohchr.org/Documen ts/Countries/AT/AustriaReport.pdf (11 February 2022).

113 Republic of Austria, BGBL. I Nr. 145/2017 – Fremdenrechtsänderungsgesetz 2017. FrÄG 2017. Österreichischer Nationalrat, 18 October 2017, NR: GP XXV IA 2285/A S. 197. BR: S. 872.

114 §80 (4) Aliens' Police Act 2005, version 2017.

115 OHCHR, "Report", 4.

116 Rechnungshof, "Follow-up", 22–23.

117 Ibid.

right coalition government, return counselling (German: *Rückkehrberatung*) was a central aspect of counselling for pre-removal detainees.[118] Three years later, detention care (German: *Schubhaftbetreuung*) was renamed in return preparation (German: *Rückkehrvorbereitung*). According to the UN Refugee Agency UNHCR, after the change, detainees were much less informed about their legal situation and ways out of it.[119] Thus, many opted for an assisted return to end a situation that they believed was hopeless.[120]

Following the influx of migrants and refugees in 2015, the number of detentions increased from 2017 to 2019, compared to 2016. Regarding detainable non-citizens whose stays had been legally terminated, the rate was high in 2017 but considerably decreased in 2019 and 2020. However, detention became more effective; between 2016 and 2018, detention ended in the detainee's actual departure in 83% of cases. While assessments of Austria's detention system by specialized organizations led to relatively good results for a couple of years, concerns are again being raised about whether the principle of proportionality is sufficiently respected.[121]

Summary and Concluding Remarks

In this paper, I analyzed one aspect of Austria's asylum system: the instrument of movement restrictions. Movement restrictions have been crucial in rendering rejected asylum seekers deportable because they facilitate the control and apprehension of these individuals.

The best-known, most invasive, and – from the state's perspective – most effective form of movement restriction is pre-removal detention. In Austria, the use of detention against rejected asylum seekers began in 1990, although the instrument had been available for a much longer period. Caught between a dominant political discourse that propagated the undesirability of refugees (e.g. discourse on economic refugee) and international law that confined the use of detention pending deportation, implementation officers have not always respected the boundaries of legal permissibility. It required the involvement of a group of critical lawyers to put Austrian detention practice on the track of legality. Toward the end of the 1990s, a new minister managed to improve the

---

118 Paier, "Zur Nicht-Akzeptanz", 123.
119 United Nations High Commissioner for Refugees Büro in Österreich, "'Monitoring' der Schubhaftsituation von Asylsuchenden" (UNHCR, 2008), https://www.refworld.org/pdfid /587896664.pdf (11 February 2022).
120 Paier, "Zur Nicht-Akzeptanz", 125–26.
121 OHCHR, "Report", 3, 17.

detention system before prematurely resigning due to the intense hostility that his approach attracted.

During the first coalition government between the conservative People's Party and the right-wing Freedom Party, the use of pre-removal detention was pushed to its limits. During a three-year policy-making process that was highly contested by a wide range of actors (including international human rights organizations, legal experts, the political opposition, activists, and even some state institutions), the instrument's scope of applicability and efficiency were increased. The process was accompanied by a discourse about fraudulent asylum seekers, which were best-represented in the government's eyes by so-called Dublin cases and asylum seekers who filed subsequent applications and experienced the greatest deterioration of rights.

Following several scandals pertaining to Austria's pre-removal detention system, EU institutions developed an interest in the detention practices of member states and an awareness of the ineffectiveness of deportation and detention. As a result, detention policy and practices in Austria slowly began to change in 2007. Attempts to prioritize lenient measures over detention and establish detention facilities for deportees separate from ordinary prisons could be observed.

In addition, the legal frameworks that regulated movement restrictions underwent a paradigm shift in 2009, when deportation-related detention was replaced by a system of obligations and restrictions as a measure of first choice, as it was deemed less invasive. However, what appeared to be a liberalization of the system was, in fact, a way to extend control to more people, as the new measures were not as closely scrutinized as detention and barely contested. Moreover, detention was not completely eliminated but rather rearranged within a system of stratification; it became relevant when softer measures were not respected or unsuccessful. Over time, other forms of imprisonment were made available to Alien Police (German: *Fremdenpolizei*), especially in cases in which immigration detention was forbidden under international and constitutional law.

After the long summer of migration, detention became more effective. Due to a changed system of detention care that focused on return counselling rather than counselling about legal options, a much higher proportion of detainees left the country following detention between 2016 and 2018 than in the past.

In conclusion, rejected asylum seekers in Austria today are confronted with a diversified and stratified system of control. The first layer of control includes several obligations and restrictions, while the second layer of control concerns breaches that are sanctioned through different forms of detention or prison sentences.

Abstracts

Migrants and Refugees from the 1960s until Today

Marcel Amoser
Forgotten "Guests": Educational migration to Austria since 1945

Migration research is currently experiencing a boom. While many studies focus on labor and refugee migration, this paper focuses on the often-neglected area of educational migration. It provides an overview of student migration to Austria from the 1960s to the 1980s. This period was characterized by three coexisting logics that continue to shape the way educational migration is dealt with today: development policy, protectionism, and internationalization. The 1960s were characterized by development policy, a high number of foreign students in relation to total enrolment, as well as the development of support structures and intensified academic knowledge production about foreign students. Against the background of the mass university of the 1970s and regulations in surrounding countries, a protectionist course was also pursued in Austria, which made access to higher education more difficult for foreign students. In the 1980s, "internationalization" finally advanced to become the central guiding idea. Against the backdrop of an increasingly competitive and business-oriented university, this set a course for dealing with foreign students that is still influential today.
Keywords: Migration, University, Austria, Education, Development Policy

Wolfgang Mueller / Hannes Leidinger / Viktor Ishchenko
"When Israel Was in Egypt's Land." Jewish Emigration from the USSR, 1968–1991

In the wake of World War II, against the backdrop of the Holocaust, the founding of the State of Israel, and at times intensely hostile discrimination against the Jewish population of the Soviet Union, the desire grew among Soviet Jews to emigrate to Palestine or Israel. Approximately 8,300 Soviet Jews emigrated be-

tween 1945 and 1968. In the détente era of the early 1970s, that number rose to nearly 35,000 a year, before declining again due to new conflicts and restrictions. Following the end of the Cold War in 1990, emigration again reached a new peak. In total, about 500,000 Jews left the Soviet Union between 1968 and 1990. Most of them traveled through Austria on the way to their new homes. Several broad overviews have been published on the situation of the Jewish population in the USSR, the Jewish exodus from the USSR, and various aspects of their transit. Nevertheless, a synthesis of these findings is still lacking, and a number of questions remain open with regard to both the Austrian and Soviet perspective of Austria's role as a transit country. On the basis of material from Austrian and Soviet archives, this article attempts to address some of these research gaps.
Keywords: Soviet Union, Israel, Austria, Jews, emigration, post-WWII history

Maximilian Graf
Humanitarianism with Limits: The Reception of Refugees from the Global South in Austria in the 1970s

The article is the first study to address the Austrian reception of refugees from the Global South in the Kreisky era on the basis of available archival sources. After a brief introductory section addressing the myth and reality of Austria's role as a Cold War refuge, it proceeds with two cases studies. The first case study addresses reactions to the military coup in Chile 1973, the subsequent interactions with the junta, and the granting of asylum for persecuted Chileans. The second case study assesses Austria's contribution to the resettlement of Indochinese refugees from "small quotas" to a broader solidarity with the so-called "boat people." Both cases illustrate general patterns in Austria's refugee policies during the Cold War and the growing importance of society and NGOs in facilitating the admission of non-European refugees. The article also demonstrates that humanitarianism had its limits, and the European approach continued to dominate Austria's Cold War asylum policies. This became evident in 1981 when the arrival of Polish refugees abruptly ended Austrian participation in global refugee resettlement. The conclusion stresses the primarily European scope of Austria's refugee policies and points to several continuities in asylum policies from the 1970s to the present day.
Keywords: Austria, Chile, Vietnam, Refugees, Cold War

Judith Welz

In the Service of Deportation: The Development of Detention and Other Forms of Movement Restrictions in the Austrian Asylum System from 1990 to 2020

This article looks into the development of pre-removal detention and other forms of movement restrictions to facilitate deportation in the context of the Austrian asylum system since the 1990s. It found that while pre-removal detention was the primary instrument used to increase the deportability of rejected asylum seekers between 1990–2005, a more diversified and stratified approach emerged after 2005. The new approach prioritized a system of obligations and restrictions over detention, however, it kept detention as an option for authorities to turn to when less invasive measures failed. After some time, the new system got expanded to asylum seekers whose asylum cases were still pending. Thus, today, a large proportion of asylum seekers whose case has been rejected or who are still awaiting decision face detention or the threat thereof.

Keywords: Deportation, Detention, Asylum, Migration

Reviews

Heinrich August Winkler, Deutungskämpfe. Der Streit um die deutsche Geschichte. Historisch-politische Essays, München: C. H. Beck 2021, 278 Seiten.

Der emeritierte Berliner Historiker Heinrich August Winkler, Jahrgang 1938, ist
einer der prominentesten und produktivsten Wissenschafter seiner Zunft – nicht
nur Deutschlands. Allein seine vierbändige und vielfach preisgekrönte „Geschichte des Westens", veröffentlicht zwischen 2009 und 2015, umfasst 4.648
stattliche Seiten. Sein neuester Band ist das Gegenteil, wiewohl die von ihm
bejahte Westbindung ebenfalls einen Fluchtpunkt einnimmt. Die „Deutungskämpfe" umfassen lediglich 278 Seiten – alle Texte sind bereits veröffentlicht
worden, dazu meist als Rezensionen, und zwar zwischen 1963 (eine Besprechung
der wahlsoziologischen Studie Rudolf Heberles über Landbevölkerung und
Nationalsozialismus) und 2021 (eine kritische Auseinandersetzung mit neueren
Studien, welche die These vom deutschen Sonderweg in Zweifel ziehen). Ist eine
Publikation der vornehmlich für den Tag verfassten kurzen Essays damit über-
flüssig? Ganz und gar nicht. Es findet sich manches Kleinod: etwa die Würdigung
von Erich Fromms Pionierstudie über Arbeiter und Angestellte am Vorabend des
„Dritten Reiches", die scharfe Abrechnung mit Sebastian Haffners „Germany:
Jekyll & Hyde" oder die faire Sicht auf Kurt Schumacher, den großen Gegen-
spieler Adenauers.

Die Texte wirken erstaunlich frisch. Der Gelehrte kommt auf den Punkt, stets
ist der rote Faden erkennbar. Obwohl die Essays zu höchst unterschiedlichen
Zeiten geschrieben sind, fällt eine erstaunliche Kontinuität in Winklers Urteilen
auf, mit gewissen Einschränkungen beim deutschen Sonderweg, den der Ver-
fasser heute nicht mehr derart massiv betont wie vor einem halben Jahrhundert.
Der auf dem rechten Flügel der Sozialdemokratie angesiedelte Historiker kann
extremen Positionen wenig abgewinnen.

Vier Aufsätze der Essaysammlung betreffen die Zeit vor 1918 (darunter eine
Kritik am deutschen Nationalismus), elf die Zeit zwischen den beiden Welt-
kriegen (u. a. ein Artikel zur ambivalenten Rolle Stalins beim Aufstieg Hitlers),
neun das geteilte Deutschland (nach Winkler hat Konrad Adenauer kein neu-
trales Gesamtdeutschland gewollt, wohl aber ein im Westen integriertes), ebenfalls neun auf die letzten 30 Jahre: Wie das „Schwarzbuch des Kommunismus"
zeige, gäbe es keinen Zweck, der Unterdrückung rechtfertige. Damit zielt der
Autor nicht nur auf Stalin und Lenin, sondern auch auf Marx.

In einigen Texten rechnet Winkler mit der radikalen Studentenbewegung
ebenso ab wie mit Positionen der Partei „Die Linke". Kritisiert wird die Ge-
schichtsklitterung der Postkommunisten, die nicht konsequent mit ihrer Vergangenheit gebrochen hätten. Ob Winkler heute seine Thesen von 1994 nach wie
vor teilt? „Zu den Errungenschaften der zweiten deutschen Demokratie gehört
der Grundkonsens, dass demokratische Parteien sich nur mit demokratischen

Parteien verbünden dürfen. Was gegenüber ‚rechts‘ gilt, muss auch gegenüber ‚links‘ verteidigt werden. Mag die PDS den Sirengesang von der ‚Einheit der Linken‘ auch noch kräftig anstimmen: Die Gemeinsamkeit der Demokraten ist ein zu teuer erkauftes Gut, als dass es auf dem Altar politischer Opportunitäten geopfert werden dürfte" (S. 201 f.). In anderen Texten knöpft er sich rechte Positionen vor. So gelten die Besitzansprüche des Hauses Hohenzollern, das nach 1945 von der sowjetischen Besatzungsmacht enteignet wurde, nicht als berechtigt. Das Ausgleichsgesetz des Jahres 1994 sieht Entschädigungen bloß dann vor, wenn die Antragsteller weder dem nationalsozialistischen noch dem kommunistischen System Vorschub geleistet haben. Winkler zufolge trifft eben das auf Kronprinz Wilhelm zu. Dieser habe 1932 beim zweiten Gang zur Präsidentschaftswahl für Hitler votiert, nicht für Hindenburg. Und nach dem 30. Januar 1933 unterstütze er das neue System, weniger aus Überzeugung, mehr aus Opportunismus. In einem anderen Artikel bescheinigt der Autor der Mehrheit des preußischen Adels dem Nationalsozialismus zugearbeitet zu haben, wobei Winkler den späteren Weg Adliger in den Widerstand, die das mit dem eigenen Leben büßen mussten, keineswegs unterschlägt.

Der Berliner Historiker hat im Zuge des deutschen „Historikerstreits" von 1986 den Begriff der „Geschichtspolitik" geprägt. Gemeint ist damit die Instrumentalisierung von Geschichte für politische Zwecke. Oft vermengen sich Geschichtspolitik und Geschichtswissenschaft. Dabei ist entgegen der Lesart Winklers die Trennung wahrlich nicht einfach. Der Streitbare hat bei den Deutungskämpfen um Deutschlands Geschichte an vorderer Stelle mitgemischt, wie nicht zuletzt diese Aufsätze erhellen: argumentativ, nicht agitatorisch.

Was sich versteht: Der Rezensent teilt nicht jedes pointierte Urteil, wie begründet es immer sein mag. So ist der kürzeste Artikel – im Umfang von gut zwei Seiten – wohl der schwächste, ein Nachruf auf Fritz Fischer. Er fällt reichlich euphemistisch aus und hinter den Forschungsstand zurück. Warum hat ihn Winkler in seine Sammlung aufgenommen, zumal angesichts später bekannt gewordener Verstrickungen Fischers in die nationalsozialistische „Wissenschaftslandschaft"? Auch der Text über die Kritik an Christopher Clark und anderen wagt sich weit vor. Diese „Revisionisten" – ein missverständlicher Begriff – spielten die Rolle des Militärs im Deutschland am Vorabend des Ersten Weltkrieges herunter. Wenn Winkler davon spricht, „die deutschen Kriegsideologien [stellten] der universalistischen Moral der westlichen Demokratien ein Denken entgegen, das aus den Tiefen der deutschen Kultur schöpfte und Normen mit weltumspannendem Anspruch wie Freiheit, Gleichheit, Brüderlichkeit zurückwies" (S. 63), fällt auf: Ein Vergleich der Politik Deutschlands mit der Politik anderer Länder unterbleibt.

Ungeachtet dessen: Die Essaysammlung gibt einen sehr guten Überblick aus der Sicht Winklers zu kontrovers beurteilten Fragen deutscher (Zeit-)Geschichte.

Sie ist mit Abkürzungs-, Anmerkungs- und Personenverzeichnis, welches das Geburts- und Todesjahr der Genannten enthält, sorgfältig gestaltet. Wer Quisquilien sucht: Die beiden Brüder Gregor und Otto Straßer schreiben sich nicht mit „ss", wie immer wieder zu lesen, selbst hier. Das Geburts- und Todesjahr des sowjetischen Diplomaten Maxim Maximowitsch Litwinow lauten: 1976–1951. Zuweilen stehen knappe Passagen den Texten voran, um deren jeweiligen Kontext besser einordnen zu können. Eine längere Einleitung, die den Stellenwert der Texte für die Gegenwart verdeutlicht, hätte dem Anliegen des Autors wohl besser entsprochen. „Glänzend geschrieben" (S. 57) – das Lob Winklers für Christopher Clark gilt auch für ihn.

Eckhard Jesse

Martin Bleckmann, Verstaatlichung und Entschädigung in Österreich. Lex Bleckmann, Wien: Verlag Österreich 2021, 880 Seiten.

Der Autor behandelt in diesem Werk die Verstaatlichung von Unternehmen in der Zweiten Republik. Zugleich beinhaltet die Schrift eine umfassende Aufarbeitung des österreichischen Enteignungsrechts. Es geht in der Monografie um einen realen Fall, der Schoeller-Bleckmann Stahlwerke AG, deren Anteile, wie die von 69 weiteren Großunternehmen, durch das Erste Verstaatlichungsgesetz 1946 verstaatlicht wurden.

Die Unternehmensgeschichte geht auf das Jahr 1862 zurück. Damals erwarben – voneinander unabhängig – zwei Industriepioniere, Heinrich Bleckmann in Mürzzuschlag und Alexander Schoeller in Ternitz, Eisen- und Stahlwerke. 1924 kam es zur Fusionierung der beiden zwischenzeitig in Aktiengesellschaften umgewandelten Unternehmen. Fortan war die Firma Schoeller-Bleckmann das zweitgrößte österreichische Montanunternehmen der Ersten Republik mit zahlreichen Dependancen auf der ganzen Welt, die – bis heute – zum Weltruf des Firmennamens beitragen. Dann 1946 die Zäsur: Einstimmig beschlossen ÖVP, SPÖ und KPÖ am 26. Juli das Verstaatlichungsgesetz, das aber erst – wegen des Einspruchs der Sowjetunion – mit Kundmachung im Bundesgesetzblatt am 17. September 1946 in Kraft trat. Damit war zeitgleich – das heißt: in dieser juristischen Sekunde – die Enteignung (Verstaatlichung) tatsächlich vollzogen.

Nicht vollzogen war die Entschädigung. Das Verstaatlichungsgesetz versprach zwar ausdrücklich eine „angemessene Entschädigung" (S. 96) und meinte damit einen, dem Verkehrswert entsprechenden Wertausgleich (§ 365 ABGB). Aber der Gesetzgeber befand, dass dazu „die näheren Vorschriften ein besonderes Bundesgesetz" treffen soll. Und dieses Gesetz – das Erste Verstaatlichungs-Entschädigungsgesetz – kam rund acht Jahre später. Zwischenzeitig hatte der Verfassungsgerichtshof (VfGH) die Verstaatlichung als „Sonderfall" (S. 156) der Enteignung qualifiziert, und zur Entschädigung festgestellt, dass nur mehr deren Fälligkeit offen sei. Davon unbeeindruckt legte das Gesetz von 1954 eine Pauschalentschädigung für die verstaatlichten Betriebe fest, was die Opposition als „Raubrittermethode" (S. 123) bezeichnete.

Der gesetzliche Widerspruch zwischen der versprochenen Angemessenheit von 1946 und der festgelegten, weit geringeren Pauschalierung von 1954 hatte zur Folge, dass Enteignete zum Teil gar nichts bekamen und manche, wie Bleckmann, einen Bruchteil. Die zwölfköpfige Familie Bleckmann klagte daher – gemeinsam mit Schoeller – den offenen Betrag bei den Zivilgerichten und danach beim VfGH ein. Doch die Gerichte gaben den Millionen-Klagen wegen Unzulässigkeit bzw. Unzuständigkeit nicht statt. Das heißt: Obwohl sich der Gesetzgeber als „unehrlicher Makler" erwies, schien gegen den „Wortbruch" (S. 176), wie es der VfGH-Richter Korn laut Beratungsprotokoll nannte, kein Kraut gewachsen.

Was folgte, war eine – im Detail im Buch von Bleckmann nachzulesende – Odyssee, die ich, um den Rahmen nicht zu sprengen, nur in Schlagworten wiedergeben kann. 1958 entschied der VfGH aufgrund der Anrufung durch drei von zwölf Mitgliedern der Familien Bleckmann, dass für den geltend gemachten Vermögensanspruch dieser drei die Zivilgerichte zuständig seien. 1959 wiesen BG und LG die Anträge von Bleckmann ab und der OGH wies den dagegen erhobenen Rekurs mit einem – unter diesen Voraussetzungen nicht als Ruhmesblatt anzusehenden – Konformitätsbeschluss zurück. Vor diesem bis dato – zumindest mir – nicht bekannten Hintergrund erhellt, warum der Gesetzgeber kurzerhand durch eine Verfassungsbestimmung in § 12 des Zweiten Verstaatlichungs-Entschädigungsgesetzes von 1959 die Grundrechte für die Entschädigungen suspendierte (!) und damit diese unanfechtbar machte.

Über 60 Jahre später meldet sich nun mit Bleckmann einer aus der dritten Generation der durch die Verstaatlichung Übervorteilten zu Wort. Warum? Ich meine, weil sich nach dem einzigartigen Missbrauch der Verfassung im Jahr 1959 zur Legitimation von einem – wie der VfGH im Erkenntnis 1957 selber sagte – „verfassungswidrigen Gesetz", gemeint ist das Erste Verstaatlichungs-Entschädigungsgesetz von 1954, die Rechtslage – sprich: der Rechtsschutz – wesentlich geändert hat. Bleckmann hebt in diesem Zusammenhang insbesondere die Einführung des Individualantrags zur Überprüfung von Gesetzen auf ihre Verfassungsmäßigkeit, die Stärkung der Grundrechte durch die Rechtsprechung und die Aufhebung der mehr als ungewöhnlichen Verfassungsbestimmung des § 12 Zweites Verstaatlichungs-Entschädigungsgesetz hervor.

Bleckmann kommt zu dem Ergebnis, dass es auch heute noch – also 86 Jahre nach der Verstaatlichung – vermögens- und namensrechtliche Ansprüche von Enteigneten bzw. deren Erben gibt. Wie er darauf kommt, welche Überlegungen und Argumente dafürsprechen, warum keine Verjährung gegeben ist, alles das und vieles mehr bilden den Schwerpunkt seiner zum Teil gutachterlichen Aufbereitung der Lex Bleckmann. Hierdurch, also durch den gutachterlichen Blickwinkel, entfernt sich leider das Werk von der Rechtswissenschaft. Theoretische Erkenntnisse und dogmatische Auseinandersetzungen kommen daher zu kurz. Stattdessen stehen im Zentrum des Buchs „Optionen" zur Geltendmachung des Vermögensanspruches (S. 287–416). Dazu kommen die – meines Erachtens sowohl die Republik als auch die Rechtsnachfolger (aufgrund der Privatisierung) betreffenden – heiklen Namensansprüche (S. 417 ff.).

Bemerkenswert ist die – m. E. zum Teil etwas detailverliebte – Analyse des VfGH-Erkenntnis 1957. Zusammenfassend schreibt Bleckmann (S. 482): „Der Beschluss des VfGH 1957 besteht aus zwei Teilen. Im ersten Teil prüfte der VfGH formal die Zulässigkeit der Klage, das heißt seine Zuständigkeit. Die „entscheidende Frage" war hierbei für den VfGH, „ob der Anspruch im ordentlichen Rechtsweg auszutragen ist". Die „Lösung der allein in Betracht kommenden Rechtsfrage" war für den VfGH „in Art. 13 des Verwaltungsentlastungsgesetzes […] enthalten". Der geltend gemachte Anspruch war daher – das heißt: weil durch Art. 13 VEG der Weg zu den Zivilgerichten über das Eisenbahnenteignungsgesetz eröffnet war – laut VfGH im ordentlichen Rechtsweg auszutragen. Der VfGH ließ dabei offen, ob der Anspruch ein privatrechtlicher ist. Im zweiten Teil des Beschlusses von 1957 sprach der VfGH – entgegen dem von der Gruppe Bleckmann erhobenen Klagegrund – aus, dass „hier ein unerfüllter Anspruch auf angemessene Entschädigung vor[liegt], für welchen lediglich eine materiellrechtliche Begründung gegeben wird". Hierbei schloss der VfGH die „Deutung" nicht aus, dass es sich um einen „Schadenersatzanspruch aus dem Titel eines verfassungswidrigen Gesetzes" handeln könnte, über welchen aber auch „der ordentliche Richter zu befinden hat".

Zwei vermögenrechtliche Optionen stechen in dem Werk besonders hervor. Zum einen die Option einer A-Klage nach Art 137 B-VG wegen Verkürzung des Anspruchs durch das wegen der Pauschalierung vom VfGH (1957) als verfassungswidrig angesehene Erste Verstaatlichungs-Entschädigungsgesetz (S. 312 ff.). Zum anderen die durch die legendären Rückübereignungserkenntnisse des VfGH im Jahr 1980 (VfSlg 8981) geschaffene Möglichkeit der Aufhebung des Ersten Verstaatlichungsgesetzes wegen Zweckverfehlung (spätestens seit der Privatisierung) und die nachfolgende (zivilgerichtliche) Geltendmachung eines Bereicherungsanspruches (S. 391 ff.). Die – wie Bleckmann konstatiert – „Gretchenfrage" dabei ist, ob der Rechtsstaat – m. E. allen voran der VfGH – dazu reif ist.

Ich kann Bleckmann folgen, dass die gesetzliche Grundlage des unerfüllten Anspruches § 1 des Ersten Verstaatlichungsgesetzes ist. Die Wurzel dieses Anspruches liegt meines Erachtens im öffentlichen Recht, nämlich in der mit der Enteignung (Verstaatlichung) zusammenhängenden Verpflichtung der Republik

Österreich (Bund) auf angemessene Entschädigung. Die gesetzliche Verpflichtung auf angemessene Entschädigung gemäß § 1 Abs. 2 des Ersten Verstaatlichungsgesetzes deckt sich mit dem Art. 5 StGG in Verbindung mit § 365 ABGB. Das Erste Verstaatlichungsgesetz war und ist daher meines Erachtens in diesem Sinn verfassungskonform.

Was die Durchdringung der Verstaatlichungsthematik betrifft, ist zu fragen, ob Bleckmann hier nicht zu weit greift, wenn er meint (S. XII): „Die Lex Bleckmann ist in diesem Buch aber nur die Spitze eines Eisberges. Die Rechtsprechung des VfGH im Zusammenhang mit Enteignungen und Entschädigungen baut auf die der Causa zugrundeliegende Entscheidung von 1957 auf. Doch diese Entscheidung erweist sich aufgrund der in dieser Arbeit aufgezeigten – und anhand von bislang unveröffentlichten Beratungsprotokollen belegten – Widersprüche als unhaltbar. Damit verlieren die Rechtsprechungsäste, die sich daraus seither entwickelt haben, ihre Grundlage. Zugleich erreicht das Werk dadurch eine Metaebene, auf der es nicht mehr bloß um Bleckmann und allenfalls weitere durch die Verstaatlichung krass Übervorteilte geht, sondern auf der es auch um eine Revision in der einschlägigen Rechtsprechung – beginnend bei Legalenteignungen und endend bei der Haftung wegen legislativen Unrechts – gehen könnte.“

Dazu ein Detail: Im Rahmen der – wie es im Vorwort heißt – 15-jährigen Recherche zu dem Werk konnte Bleckmann im Staatsarchiv Einblick in die 50 Jahre unter Verschluss gehaltenen Prozessakte seiner Vorfahren nehmen. Diesem Umstand verdankt er dem seit 2000 geltenden Bundesarchivgesetz. Damit wurde der überfällige „Zugang zum Archivgut des Bundes für die Wissenschaft und die Bürger" (so die Erläuterungen zum Gesetz) geschaffen. Die in den Akten unter Verschluss gehaltenen Protokolle und Entscheidungsentwürfe entpuppten sich offenbar als wahre Fundgrube. Darin war, wie oben zitiert, vom „Wortbruch des Gesetzgebers" und dem seinen Vorfahren widerfahrenen „Unrecht" die (richterliche) Rede. Umso erstaunlicher ist für mich, dass die Richter nicht schon damals getreu der Radbruchschen Formel entschieden haben.

Kritisch sind m. E. die Ausführungen von Bleckmann zur Höhe des Vermögensanspruches zu hinterfragen. Bleckmann geht dabei von einem – aus dem Liegenschafts(enteignungs)recht abgeleiteten – konservativen Ansatz aus. Im Wesentlichen beschränkt er sich auf das 1957 eingeklagte Kapital samt Zinsen und Valorisierung. Nur am Rande bringt er als „Zinsschaden" eine durch den verfassungswidrigen § 12 Zweites Verstaatlichungs-Entschädigungsgesetz bedingt gewesene Unanfechtbarkeit ins Spiel. Das mag zwar alles billig, aber nicht gerecht sein. Meines Erachtens übersieht Bleckmann hierbei aber, dass ein Unternehmen wie ein lebender Organismus ist und dass daher hier – wie in der Betriebswirtschaft üblich – auch Referenzwertmethoden zur Feststellung der Anspruchshöhe zu berücksichtigen sind.

Resümee: Das Werk „Verstaatlichung und Entschädigung in Österreich" des renommierten Rechtswissenschafters und gelernten Rechtsanwalts Bleckmann gibt interessante Einblicke in eine ganz besondere Enteignungsthematik. Der Autor nimmt anhand bisheriger Geschehnisse die Fährte in der Lex Bleckmann auf, zeigt, wie sich die Großparteien an der Verstaatlichung und deren Günstlinge an der Privatisierung (ab 1993) hemmungslos bereicherten, und wie die Enteigneten aufgrund willkürlicher Ungerechtigkeit „durch die Finger schauten". Was bleibt, ist ein offengelegter Makel des Rechtsstaates, verursacht durch Rechtsbeugung und Rechtsbruch. Wir, die Bürger dieses Staates, sollten uns daher im Klaren sein, dass irgendwann – und Zeit ist schon genug vergangen – auch dieser Fleck bereinigt werden sollte. Denn wie der Zeithistoriker Oliver Rathkolb im Schlusswort festhält: Die Verstaatlichung war ein fehlgeschlagenes Experiment mit schweren rechtlichen Fehlern. Ich rege daher – wie bereits im Österreichischen Anwaltsblatt 2021 (600) zu „100 Jahre Republik Österreich" – an, ja ich plädiere, dass sich endlich wirkliche Persönlichkeiten bei den entscheidenden Instanzen dieses himmelschreienden „Unrechts" (O-Ton des VfGH-Richters Dr. Korn) annehmen und die schweren Versäumnisse in der Vergangenheit rund um die miese Entschädigung bei der Verstaatlichten nicht länger tatenlos hinnehmen.

Nikolaus Lehner

Peter Black / Béla Rásky / Marianne Windsperger (Hg.), Collaboration in Eastern Europe during the Second World war and the Holocaust (Beiträge des VWI zur Holocaustforschung 7), Wien/Hamburg: New Academic Press 2019, 384 Seiten.

Der Band, der auf eine bereits 2013 vom Wiener Wiesenthal-Institut veranstaltete Konferenz zurückgeht, versucht sich, so die HerausgeberInnen in ihrem Vorwort, an einer Zwischenbilanz zu „Komplizenschaft und Kollaboration" (S. 12) mit dem NS-Regime in Osteuropa während des Zweiten Weltkrieges. Die Beschäftigung damit sei, so die HerausgeberInnen, „nach einigen kurzen und brutalen Gefühlsaufwallungen, aber auch Versuchen einer Rechtsprechung in der unmittelbaren Nachkriegszeit" (S. 12) über Jahrzehnte lang verunmöglicht worden. Die Gründe für das Beschweigen waren vielschichtig: Der deutsche Vernichtungskrieg betraf in weiten Teilen Osteuropas nicht nur Juden und Roma, sondern auch den Großteil der Bevölkerungen in einer ganz anderen Dimension als im „Westen" und lenkte nach 1945 die Aufmerksamkeit auf Verfolgung und Widerstand. Die Verstrickungen in den Völkermord an Juden und Roma wurden von den volksdemokratischen und KP-Regimes zugunsten einer harmonisie-

renden Erzählung von widerständigen Völkern nicht thematisiert, stattdessen
einige „Verräter" als „Volks"- und „Klassenfeinde" identifiziert und aus den
nationalen (Opfer-)Gemeinschaften ausgeschlossen. Beim tschechischen Beispiel waren dies einzelne Journalisten, die Vorkriegs-Faschisten oder auch Teile
der Protektoratsregierung, nicht jedoch die Sicherheitskräfte im Protektorat
Böhmen und Mähren, die u. a. an der Verfolgung von Juden, Roma und
ZwangsarbeiterInnen wesentlichen Anteil hatten und denen sich Alfons Adam
(S. 127–149) widmet.

Während in Westeuropa die Frage nach der Mittäterschaft ab den 1980er-
Jahren gestellt wurde, hatte Osteuropa nach dem Fall der KP-Diktaturen „viel
mehr zu erinnern und zu vergessen als Westeuropa 1945" (S. 14). Zu den Opfern
des NS-Regimes traten die der kommunistischen Diktaturen, die den Gesellschaften zeitlich und mental näher lagen. Nicht zuletzt aus diesen verschiedenen
Opfernarrativen wächst das tiefe Unverständnis, das den „Osten" auch mehr als
dreißig Jahre nach 1989 vom „Westen" nicht nur geschichtspolitisch trennt.

Der Band ist inhaltlich wie geographisch sehr breit konzipiert. Der inhaltliche
Bogen spannt sich von „Kollaboration und Repressionsapparate" über „Admi-
nistrativ und institutionalisierte Kollaboration", „lokale und regionale Aspekte"
bis hin zu zwei Beiträgen zur Verfolgung der Roma und zur Aufarbeitung der
Kollaboration nach 1945. So verschieden wie die Beiträge war auch der Status der
vorgestellten Länder und Gesellschaften während der NS-Zeit, von der Militär-
verwaltung über eine Aufsichtsverwaltung bei zumindest theoretischer Auto-
nomie, bis hin zur völligen Absenz eigener staatlicher Strukturen. Dazu kamen
die mit dem Reich verbündeten Staaten Kroatien und Bulgarien. So unter-
schiedlich die Regimes auch waren, so waren sie doch alle in die Vernichtung des
europäischen Judentums eingebunden. Die Studien behandeln diese Einbindung
auf Ebene der zentralen staatlichen Institutionen, jedoch meist auch einzelner
staatlicher oder nichtstaatlicher Akteure und verlagern so den Blick verdien-
terweise auf eine Mikroebene, die neben den Taten und Tätern auch die Aus-
leuchtung ihrer Motive und Handlungsspielräume ermöglicht. Hier sei etwa der
Beitrag von Tomasz Frydel genannt, der unter dem Titel „Ordinary Men?" die
polnische „Blaue Polizei" im Karpatenvorland des „Generalgouvernements" als
Tätergeschichte konzipiert (S.69–126). Bei den polnischen Polizisten hätte es sich
viel eher um „gewöhnliche Männer" gehandelt als bei dem von Christopher
Browning unter dem gleichen Titel in seiner bekannten Studie behandelten
deutschen Reserve-Polizeibataillon 101. Frydel stützt seine These auf die „dichte
Beschreibung" des Wirkens von siebzig Polizeibeamten im östlichen Teil des
Distrikts Krakau. Schrittweise wuchsen den aus der polnischen Vorkriegspolizei
rekrutierten Einheiten neben ihrer Funktion als Ordnungsmacht neue Aufgaben
zu, von der Kontrolle der Lebensmittelabgaben bis hin zur Liquidation jüdischer
Ghettos, der Jagd nach untergetauchten Verfolgten und der teilweisen Teilnahme

an Erschießungen. Dabei standen sie nicht nur unter der Befehlsgewalt und den Loyalitätsansprüchen der deutschen Organe, sondern auch des polnischen Untergrundstaates. Weit mehr als ideologische Präpositionen bestimmten pragmatische Prämissen und situative Notwendigkeiten und Zwänge ihr Handeln, sodass sie letztlich „nicht Herren ihres eigenen Schicksals" gewesen seien (S. 118).

Der Zugang von Filip Erdeljac ragt aus den TäterInnen-zentrierten Beiträgen hervor. Erdeljac untersucht unter dem Titel „Also a mother to us Jews" (S. 223–242) an die Organe des kroatischen Ustascha-Staates – mit Staatsführer Ante Pavelić an der Spitze – gerichtete Briefe kroatischer Juden, die in der Zwischenkriegszeit in der kroatischen Nationalbewegung tätig waren und vom jugoslawischen Staat verfolgt wurden, ihren Ausschluss aus der neuen nationalen Gemeinschaft nicht verstanden und dagegen mit dem Hinweis auf ihr „Kroatentum" protestierten.

Die Texte von Leszek Gorycki und Slawomir Kapralski (S. 297–316) sowie Daniel Vojak (S. 317–344) widmen sich der Verfolgung und Ermordung der Roma in Polen respektive Kroatien und bieten so gute Vergleichsmöglichkeiten. Noch viel weniger als die Vernichtung der Juden waren die Verfolgung und Ermordung der Roma in Osteuropa Thema und werden noch immer verschwiegen oder wie in Tschechien verharmlost (Adam, S. 127).

Insgesamt bietet der Band einen guten Überblick, auch wenn eine etwas stringentere Auswahl der Texte möglich gewesen wäre – Griechenland etwa hatte keine KP-Vergangenheit, hingegen fehlt die Slowakei. Aber die Geschichte der Kollaboration ist wie die Osteuropas ein weites Feld und der Band eröffnet wichtige Erkenntnisse und bietet wertvolle Anregungen für die weitere Forschung.

Niklas Perzi

Ljiljana Radonić, **Der Zweite Weltkrieg in postsozialistischen Gedenkmuseen. Geschichtspolitik zwischen der „Anrufung Europas" und dem Fokus auf „unser" Leid** (Medien und kulturelle Erinnerung 6), Berlin/Boston: De Gruyter 2021, 327 Seiten.

Unter dem Titel „Der Zweite Weltkrieg in Post-Sozialistischen Gedenkmuseen" präsentiert Ljiljana Radonić eine umfassende vergleichende Darstellung von staatlich finanzierten postsozialistischen Gedenkmuseen, die nach 1989 eröffnet oder erneut eröffnet wurden. Im Zentrum der Auseinandersetzung steht die Frage, wie die Periode des Zweiten Weltkriegs in den elf postsozialistischen EU-Mitgliedsländern in den Museen auf visueller sowie auch auf narrativer Ebene repräsentiert wird. Der Untersuchungszeitraum gibt zwar auch Einblicke in die sozialistische Ära, umfasst jedoch vornehmlich die Zeit nach der Wende; denn gerade die EU-Beitrittsbemühungen der jeweiligen Länder lassen ein verstärktes Aushandeln von Geschichte innerhalb der Museen erkennen und bilden damit einen zentralen Punkt innerhalb der Untersuchung. Auf den ersten Blick könnte angenommen werden, dass die Publikation die Ausstellungsgeschichte der postsozialistischen Museen skizziert, doch die Publikation geht einen entscheidenden Schritt weiter und unternimmt den Versuch, Museumsgruppierungen auf Grundlage gemeinsamer übergeordneter Narrative und Darstellungsformen vorzunehmen. Eines der wichtigsten Ergebnisse der umfassenden Untersuchung ist, dass die jeweiligen Geschichtserzählungen zwischen zwei Polen oszillieren.

Der eine Pol von Museen betreibt etwas, das Ljiljana Radonić als „Anrufung Europas" bezeichnet. Diese allesamt staatlich finanzierten Institutionen, wie das Jasenovac-Gedenkmuseum in Kroatien, das Museum des Slowakischen Nationalaufstands und das Holocaust-Gedenkzentrum in Budapest übernehmen nach Radonić Ästhetiken westlicher Holocaustmuseen und setzen den Fokus mehr auf das individuelle Opfer, als auf das Kollektiv. Diese Gruppe an Museen versucht, sich an die „internationalen Vorgaben" anzupassen, um damit den vermeintlichen europäischen Standards zu entsprechen. Auffällig ist jedoch dabei, dass es vor allem nicht-europäische „Memorial Museums" sind, an denen sich die Museen orientieren, um ihr „Europäischsein" hervorzuheben. Das United States Holocaust Museum in Washington sowie auch die Gedenkstätte Yad Vashem in Jerusalem fungieren dabei als grundlegende Gestaltungsvorlagen, an denen sich die europäischen Museen in Osteuropa abarbeiten. Ein Beispiel stellt die „Bilderwand" in Yad Vashem oder auch der „Tower of Faces" im United States Holocaust Museum dar, welche sich auch in den europäischen Museen in abgewandelter Form wiederfindet. Damit lässt sich u. a. feststellen, dass die ästhetische Ausrichtung dieser Museen auch die Universalisierung der Holocaust-Darstellung in Umlauf bringt. Dieser Art von globalen Ausstellungstendenzen lohnt es sich, in weiterer Folge nachzugehen, da bisher kaum Forschungsliteratur in diesem Zusammenhang besteht.

Den anderen Pol bilden Museen und ihre RepräsentantInnen, die Europa dazu herausfordern, die Leiden unter dem Kommunismus, der Sowjetunion bzw. dem Stalinismus anzuerkennen. Zu dieser Gruppe zählen das Museum der Okkupation im estnischen Tallinn, das Museum der Okkupation Lettlands in Riga, das Museum der Genozidopfer in Vilnius sowie das Haus des Terrors in Budapest. Inszenierungstaktiken, die Parallelen zwischen den Symboliken des Kommunismus und des Nationalsozialismus herstellen, werden sowohl auf bildhafter als auch auf narrativer Ebene in dieser Gruppe angewandt: Zwei übergroße Porträts von Hitler und Stalin finden sich bspw. am Anfang der Ausstellung im Museum der Okkupation Lettlands. Auf dem Gebäude vom Haus des Terrors ragt den Betrachtenden ein Dachsims aus Pfeilkreuzen und Sternen entgegen. Im

Tallinner Museum fanden sich bis zur Umgestaltung im Jahr 2018 zwei stilisierte Lokomotiven mit Hakenkreuz- und Stern-Symbol wieder. Diese narrativen und bildhaften Vergleiche münden nach Radonić schlussendlich darin, dass alle drei Museen im Verlauf der Ausstellung die NS-Besatzung als weniger schlimm und die sowjetischen Verbrechen als das größere Übel darstellen.

Nicht verwunderlich ist somit, dass die Thematisierung sowie auch die Darstellung der nationalsozialistischen Besatzung und der Holocaust in den drei Museen sehr reduziert wiedergegeben werden, um der eigenen Opfererzählung nicht den narrativen sowie visuellen Raum zu nehmen. Problematisch wird von Radonić auch die Überschreibung von Objekten mit neuen Inhalten gesehen. Der Koffer, der in Holocaustmuseen stellvertretend für die deportierten Juden steht, zeigt in eindringlicher Weise, wie symbolbehaftete Objekte in den erwähnten postsozialistischen Gedenkmuseen neu besetzt werden, indem dieser auch für Personen verwendet wird, die beispielsweise in den Gulag transportiert wurden.

Aus der Publikation wird deutlich, dass hier eine analytische Trennung zwischen den Inhalten, die den Sozialismus und jene, welche die nationalsozialistische Besatzung und den Holocaust betreffen, nicht zielführend wäre. Zu sehr sind die zeitperiodischen Stränge und die daraus resultierenden Ereignisse miteinander verwoben. Gerade das Herausarbeiten dieser Verbindungslinien stellt einen wichtigen Mehrwert dar, um sich ein übergeordnetes Bild dieser zum Teil recht heterogenen Landschaft von Gedenkmuseen und deren Vermittlungsziele zu verschaffen. Darunter fällt auch die sorgfältige Analyse der visuellen Objekte. Wie in der Publikation betont wird, ist die politische Einflussnahme mit der visuellen Gestaltung eng verbunden.

Der daran anknüpfende Versuch, global verzweigte Ausstellungstaktiken aufzufächern, stellt somit einen wichtigen Mehrwert dar, den Radonić in ihrem zukünftigen Forschungsprojekt „Globalisierte Gedenkmuseen" ausbauen wird. Ein Team von LänderexpertInnen wird im Zusammenhang mit der Forschungsarbeit fünfzig Museen auf vier Kontinenten erforschen, und weitere Schlüsse über die global vernetzte Gestaltung von Museen und deren länderspezifischen Vermittlungsvorstellungen ziehen und diese Vernetzungen offenlegen.

Klaudija Sabo

Authors

Marcel Amoser, Mag. BA MA
University assistant at the Department of Contemporary History at the University of Innsbruck and a member of the doctoral program "Dynamics of Inequality and Difference in the Age of Globalization", marcel.amoser@uibk.ac.at

Maximilian Graf, Dr.
Research Fellow in the ERC project "Unlikely refuge? Refugees and citizens in East-Central Europe in the 20th century", affiliated with the Masaryk Institute and Archives of the Czech Academy of Sciences, graf@mua.cas.cz

Viktor Ishchenko, Prof. Dr.
Deputy Director of the Institute of General History at the Russian Academy of Sciences in Moscow

Eckhard Jesse, Univ.-Prof. Dr.
Institut für Politikwissenschaft, TU Chemnitz, eckhard.jesse@phil.tu-chemnitz.de

Nikolaus Lehner, Prof. Dr.
Em. Rechtsanwalt, Wien, nikolaus.lehner@inode.at

Hannes Leidinger, Mag. Dr. Privatdoz.
Lecturer at the Department of Contemporary History of the University of Vienna, and the head of the Vienna office of the Ludwig-Boltzmann-Instituts für Kriegsfolgenforschung, hannes.leidinger@univie.ac.at

Wolfgang Mueller, Univ.-Prof. Mag. Dr.
Professor for Russian History at the University of Vienna and Deputy Head of its Institute of East European History, w.mueller@univie.ac.at

Niklas Perzi, Dr.
Zentrum für Historische Migrationsforschung im Institut für Geschichte des
ländlichen Raums, niklas.perzi@migrationsforschung.at

Dirk Rupnow, Univ.-Prof. Mag. Dr.
Dean of the Faculty of Philosophy and History of the University of Innsbruck,
Dirk.Rupnow@uibk.ac.at

Klaudija Sabo, Dr., MA
Forschungs- und Lehrbereich Visuelle Kultur, Institut für Kulturanalyse, Alpen-
Adria-Universität Klagenfurt, Klaudija.Sabo@aau.at

Judith Welz, MA
PhD-student at the Department of Contemporary History of the University of
Innsbruck, Judith.Welz@student.uibk.ac.at

Zitierregeln

Bei der Einreichung von Manuskripten, über deren Veröffentlichung im Laufe eines doppelt anonymisierten Peer Review Verfahrens entschieden wird, sind unbedingt die Zitierregeln einzuhalten. Unverbindliche Zusendungen von Manuskripten als word-Datei an: agnes.meisinger@univie.ac.at

I. Allgemeines

Abgabe: elektronisch in Microsoft Word DOC oder DOCX.

Textlänge: 60.000 Zeichen (inklusive Leerzeichen und Fußnoten), Times New Roman, 12 Punkt, 1 $\frac{1}{2}$-zeilig. Zeichenzahl für Rezensionen 6.000–8.200 Zeichen (inklusive Leerzeichen).

Rechtschreibung: Grundsätzlich gilt die Verwendung der neuen Rechtschreibung mit Ausnahme von Zitaten.

II. Format und Gliederung

Kapitelüberschriften und – falls gewünscht – Unterkapiteltitel deutlich hervorheben mittels Nummerierung. Kapitel mit römischen Ziffern [I. Literatur], Unterkapitel mit arabischen Ziffern [1.1 Dissertationen] nummerieren, maximal bis in die dritte Ebene untergliedern [1.1.1 Philologische Dissertationen]. Keine Interpunktion am Ende der Gliederungstitel.

Keine Silbentrennung, linksbündig, Flattersatz, keine Leerzeilen zwischen Absätzen, keine Einrückungen; direkte Zitate, die länger als vier Zeilen sind, in einem eigenen Absatz (ohne Einrückung, mit Gänsefüßchen am Beginn und Ende).

Zahlen von null bis zwölf ausschreiben, ab 13 in Ziffern. Tausender mit Interpunktion: 1.000. Wenn runde Zahlen wie zwanzig, hundert oder dreitausend nicht in unmittelbarer Nähe zu anderen Zahlenangaben in einer Textpassage aufscheinen, können diese ausgeschrieben werden.

Daten ausschreiben: „1930er" oder „1960er-Jahre" statt „30er" oder „60er Jahre".

Datumsangaben: In den Fußnoten: 4.3.2011 [keine Leerzeichen nach den Punkten, auch nicht 04.03.2011 oder 4. März 2011]; im Text das Monat ausschreiben [4. März 2011].

Personennamen im Fließtext bei der Erstnennung immer mit Vor- und Nachnamen.

Namen von Organisationen im Fließtext: Wenn eindeutig erkennbar ist, dass eine Organisation, Vereinigung o. Ä. vorliegt, können die Anführungszeichen weggelassen werden: „Die Gründung des Österreichischen Alpenvereins erfolgte 1862." „Als Mitglied im

Womens Alpine Club war ihr die Teilnahme gestattet." **Namen von Zeitungen/Zeitschriften** etc. siehe unter „Anführungszeichen".

Anführungszeichen im Fall von Zitaten, Hervorhebungen und bei Erwähnung von Zeitungen/Zeitschriften, Werken und Veranstaltungstiteln im Fließtext immer doppelt: „"

Einfache Anführungszeichen nur im Fall eines Zitats im Zitat: „Er sagte zu mir: ‚...."

Klammern: Gebrauchen Sie bitte generell runde Klammern, außer in Zitaten für Auslassungen: […] und Anmerkungen: [Anm. d. A.].

Formulieren Sie **bitte geschlechtsneutral bzw. geschlechtergerecht.** Verwenden Sie im ersteren Fall bei Substantiven das Binnen-I („ZeitzeugInnen"), nicht jedoch in Komposita („Bürgerversammlung" statt „BürgerInnenversammlung").

Darstellungen und Fotos als eigene Datei im jpg-Format (mind. 300 dpi) einsenden. Bilder werden schwarz-weiß abgedruckt; die Rechte an den abgedruckten Bildern sind vom Autor/von der Autorin einzuholen. Bildunterschriften bitte kenntlich machen: Abb.: Spanische Reiter auf der Ringstraße (Quelle: Bildarchiv, ÖNB).

Abkürzungen: Bitte Leerzeichen einfügen: vor % oder €/zum Beispiel z. B./unter anderem u. a.

Im Text sind möglichst wenige allgemeine Abkürzungen zu verwenden.

III.   Zitation

Generell keine Zitation im Fließtext, auch keine Kurzverweise. Fußnoten immer mit einem Punkt abschließen.

Die nachfolgenden Hinweise beziehen sich auf das Erstzitat von Publikationen.
Bei weiteren Erwähnungen sind Kurzzitate zu verwenden.
- Wird hintereinander aus demselben Werk zitiert, bitte den Verweis **Ebd./ebd.** bzw. mit anderer Seitenangabe **Ebd., 12./ebd., 12.** gebrauchen (kein Ders./Dies.), analog: Vgl. ebd.; vgl. ebd., 12.
- Zwei Belege in einer Fußnote mit einem **Strichpunkt;** trennen: Gehmacher, Jugend, 311; Dreidemy, Kanzlerschaft, 29.
- Bei Übernahme von direkten Zitaten aus der Fachliteratur **Zit. n./zit. n.** verwenden.
- Indirekte Zitate werden durch **Vgl./vgl.** gekennzeichnet.

Monografien: Vorname und Nachname, Titel, Ort und Jahr, Seitenangabe [ohne „S."].

Beispiel Erstzitat: Johanna Gehmacher, Jugend ohne Zukunft. Hitler-Jugend und Bund Deutscher Mädel in Österreich vor 1938, Wien 1994, 311.

Beispiel Kurzzitat: Gehmacher, Jugend, 311.
Bei mehreren AutorInnen/HerausgeberInnen: Dachs/Gerlich/Müller (Hg.), Politiker, 14.

Reihentitel: Claudia Hoerschelmann, Exilland Schweiz. Lebensbedingungen und Schicksale österreichischer Flüchtlinge 1938 bis 1945 (Veröffentlichungen des Ludwig-

Boltzmann-Institutes für Geschichte und Gesellschaft 27), Innsbruck/Wien [bei mehreren Ortsangaben Schrägstrich ohne Leerzeichen] 1997, 45.

Dissertation: Thomas Angerer, Frankreich und die Österreichfrage. Historische Grundlagen und Leitlinien 1945–1955, phil. Diss., Universität Wien 1996, 18–21 [keine ff. und f. für Seitenangaben, von–bis mit Gedankenstich ohne Leerzeichen].

Diplomarbeit: Lucile Dreidemy, Die Kanzlerschaft Engelbert Dollfuß' 1932–1934, Dipl. Arb., Université de Strasbourg 2007, 29.

Ohne AutorIn, nur HerausgeberIn: Beiträge zur Geschichte und Vorgeschichte der Julirevolte, hg. im Selbstverlag des Bundeskommissariates für Heimatdienst, Wien 1934, 13.

Unveröffentlichtes Manuskript: Günter Bischof, Lost Momentum. The Militarization of the Cold War and the Demise of Austrian Treaty Negotiations, 1950–1952 (unveröffentlichtes Manuskript), 54–55. Kopie im Besitz des Verfassers.

Quellenbände: Foreign Relations of the United States, 1941, vol. II, hg. v. United States Department of States, Washington 1958.
[nach Erstzitation mit der gängigen Abkürzung: FRUS fortfahren].

Sammelwerke: Herbert Dachs/Peter Gerlich/Wolfgang C. Müller (Hg.), Die Politiker. Karrieren und Wirken bedeutender Repräsentanten der Zweiten Republik, Wien 1995.

Beitrag in Sammelwerken: Michael Gehler, Die österreichische Außenpolitik unter der Alleinregierung Josef Klaus 1966–1970, in: Robert Kriechbaumer/Franz Schausberger/Hubert Weinberger (Hg.), Die Transformation der österreichischen Gesellschaft und die Alleinregierung Klaus (Veröffentlichung der Dr.-Wilfried Haslauer-Bibliothek, Forschungsinstitut für politisch-historische Studien 1), Salzburg 1995, 251–271, 255–257.
[bei Beiträgen grundsätzlich immer die Gesamtseitenangabe zuerst, dann die spezifisch zitierten Seiten].

Beiträge in Zeitschriften: Florian Weiß, Die schwierige Balance. Österreich und die Anfänge der westeuropäischen Integration 1947–1957, in: Vierteljahrshefte für Zeitgeschichte 42 (1994) 1, 71–94.
[Zeitschrift Jahrgang/Bandangabe ohne Beistrichtrennung und die Angabe der Heftnummer oder der Folge hinter die Klammer ohne Komma].

Presseartikel: Titel des Artikels, Zeitung, Datum, Seite.
Der Ständestaat in Diskussion, Wiener Zeitung, 5. 9. 1946, 2.

Archivalien: Bericht der Österr. Delegation bei der Hohen Behörde der EGKS, Zl. 2/pol/57, Fritz Kolb an Leopold Figl, 19. 2. 1957. Österreichisches Staatsarchiv (ÖStA), Archiv der Republik (AdR), Bundeskanzleramt (BKA)/AA, II-pol, International 2 c, Zl. 217.301-pol/57 (GZl. 215.155-pol/57); Major General Coleman an Kirkpatrick, 27. 6. 1953. The National Archives (TNA), Public Record Office (PRO), Foreign Office (FO) 371/103845, CS 1016/205 [prinzipiell zuerst das Dokument mit möglichst genauer Bezeichnung, dann das Archiv, mit Unterarchiven, -verzeichnissen und Beständen; bei weiterer Nennung der Archive bzw. Unterarchive können die Abkürzungen verwendet werden].

Internetquellen: Autor so vorhanden, Titel des Beitrags, Institution, URL: (abgerufen Datum). Bitte mit rechter Maustaste den Hyperlink entfernen, so dass der Link nicht mehr blau unterstrichen ist.

Yehuda Bauer, How vast was the crime, Yad Vashem, URL: http://www1.yadvashem.org/yv/en/holocaust/about/index.asp (abgerufen 28.2.2011).

Film: Vorname und Nachname des Regisseurs, Vollständiger Titel, Format [z. B. 8 mm, VHS, DVD], Spieldauer [Film ohne Extras in Minuten], Produktionsort/-land Jahr, Zeit [Minutenangabe der zitierten Passage].

Luis Buñuel, Belle de jour, DVD, 96 min., Barcelona 2001, 26:00–26:10 min.

Interview: InterviewpartnerIn, InterviewerIn, Datum des Interviews, Provenienz der Aufzeichnung.

Interview mit Paul Broda, geführt von Maria Wirth, 26.10.2014, Aufnahme bei der Autorin.

Die englischsprachigen Zitierregeln sind online verfügbar unter: https://www.verein-zeitgeschichte.univie.ac.at/fileadmin/user_upload/p_verein_zeitgeschichte/zg_Zitierregeln_engl_2018.pdf

Es können nur jene eingesandten Aufsätze Berücksichtigung finden, die sich an die Zitierregeln halten!

Patterns and Foundations for the Return of Authoritarian Movements in Europe

Florian Kührer-Wielach and Oliver Rathkolb (eds.)

Authoritarian Regimes in the Long Twentieth Century

Preconditions, Structures, Continuities – Contributions to European Historical Dictatorship and Transformation Research

zeitgeschichte Sonderheft

2022. 208 Seiten, kartoniert
€ 35,– D / € 36,– A
ISBN 978-3-8471-1502-1

This special issue of the journal "zeitgeschichte" presents the results of the doctoral theses written within the framework of the "Doctoral College European Historical Dictatorship and Transformation Research" (2009–2012) as selected scholarly essays. The contributions are devoted to authoritarian regimes of the 20th century in Austria, Belarus, Greece, Hungary, Italy, Latvia, Lithuania, Poland, Portgal, Romania, Spain, and the Soviet Union. Using various methods from the humanities and social sciences, different aspects of mainly "small" dictatorships are examined: conditions of emergence, structures, continuities, as well as preceding and subsequent processes of political and social transformation.

Vandenhoeck & Ruprecht Verlage

V&R unipress   www.vandenhoeck-ruprecht-verlage.com